From Finland

Kaisu Cornish

This is a true story

Perfect
Publishers Ltd

ISBN 978-1-905399-96-3

Cover design by Duncan Bamford
http://www.insightillustration.co.uk

PERFECT PUBLISHERS LTD
23 Maitland Avenue
Cambridge
CB4 1TA
England
http://www.perfectpublishers.co.uk

Disclaimer

All personal events contained within this book are true. However, some names of people mentioned have been changed to protect their identities. Some circumstances have also been changed or omitted for the same reason.

The author does not take responsibility for the opinions expressed by anyone else in this book, nor does the author take legal responsibility if anyone mentioned within the book voluntarily chooses to reveal their identity, or if any other individuals choose to reveal the identity of anyone mentioned herein to the media or otherwise. Indeed, if anyone recognises themselves from the actions described within this book, then that in itself is an admission of culpability.

In addition, any outside source, whether an individual or media source, takes full responsibility for the accuracy, timeliness and nature of anything said or published following the publication of this book. Neither the author of this book, or the publisher take responsibility for anything said, claimed or published by a third party following the publication of this book.

No material from this book may be copied, reproduced, republished, uploaded, posted, transmitted, quoted, or distributed in any way without the express permission of the author of this book.

Part One

Chapter 1

It was a moment's decision – made without any thought of the consequences – that prompted me say to Mrs Pirhonen: "I'll go! Yes – I'll go to England!"

My dear neighbour had been telling me that her nieces were in England, working as au pairs for an old lady in a big house, but they wanted to come back home to Finland after only six months. Mrs Pirhonen asked if I knew someone who could take their place.

That's when I decided, there and then, that I would be the one. There was nothing to stop me, so why shouldn't I go while I had the chance? After all, it would only be for a year.

It was October 1952 and I was confident of getting a year's leave from my job with a marine insurance firm in Helsinki. I'd already worked there for nearly four years, and it would help me do my job better if I could learn English properly.

I had no other ties. I had lost my family and my home in two separate bombings during the Finno-Russian war. The first time was in Viipuri, where I'd lived most of my young life, and the second was in Turku, where we'd escaped to be near my father's relatives.

I had no true boyfriend. I suppose I was sadly coming to terms with the fact that I'd got to the age of 28 without finding someone to love. I did have a boyfriend with whom I went to the cinema, walking, skiing, cycling, or – once – to Copenhagen. And I had another with whom to go sailing in the summer. But now I was ready for a change, and to accept the challenge that had presented itself to me.

Mrs Pirhonen was delighted by my response, both for my sake and also because she'd so easily found a replacement au pair for her nieces. They wanted to come back to complete their English studies at Helsinki University.

When they heard that I'd be replacing them in England, they asked to stay for another month, so they could experience the English way of celebrating Christmas. This suited me well, as it left me with more than a month to prepare for my year abroad.

I was living in a flat in an old part of Helsinki, with solid, grand buildings in the style of the previous century. The flat was owned by a cultured but slightly eccentric doctor's widow, Mrs Rytkola. Both her children were doctors – they were married and lived away from home, so she had let their rooms to three girls. I had the smallest room – the old study – which I thought was the nicest, particularly as it was just across the hall from the kitchen quarters, where I could entertain my friends. I'd been happy and carefree in my flat.

In war-torn Finland, where no new buildings had been constructed in the previous 10 years, it provided luxurious accommodation. For some years, people weren't allowed to keep large flats just for themselves; they had to take in tenants of their choice to share the space, or otherwise the government would let the extra rooms to any Karelian refugees.

In those days, Finland was very poor as a consequence of paying off the enormous war debts to the Russians. It was a debt of such enormity that Winston Churchill told Stalin it was far too burdensome for such a small country to be able to survive. Stalin replied that it had to be that large because he didn't want Finland to survive. But no price is too high for freedom. As a nation, we worked and worked, and for five years after the war we went short of everything. But we survived – just.

The war to defend ourselves against the Russian invaders had left us all so poor that travel abroad for ordinary people was out of the question for several years.

I had been lucky to have worked in Sweden for a year – now that I had the opportunity of going to England, I was doubly lucky.

My desirable little room was easily re-let, to a girlfriend. I knew that it would be more difficult to get my company to agree to give me a year's study leave in England, particularly as it was only two years since I'd spent a year in Sweden. But to my surprise and joy, they were delighted with the idea. They even decided not to take on a permanent replacement for me, so they could keep my job open for my return.

My destination in England was Birmingham. The house was apparently very large, and the owner – Mrs Helen Dixon – was 76 years old and lived there alone.

Mrs Pirhonen's nieces were the first two Finnish girls to live in the house, after the housekeeper had left and the other maids had retired in their old age.

My application for the job of au pair, together with a carefully-chosen and not too flattering photograph of myself, was soon in the post. The answer came just as rapidly, welcoming me to the house and telling me that I would be joining a German girl who was arriving the same week.

Mrs Dixon said she was sorry to lose her Finnish girls far too soon, and promised to take care of me. It was obvious she saw us as her children.

It was my uncle who suggested that I should travel to England on board a ship, owned by a distant relation, that was due to be delivering a cargo of timber to London. It meant I would be in safe hands on my first venture into the big wide world. The captain was a friend of my uncle, and he promised to deliver me safely to my destination.

With everything organised, I could now go to my aunt and uncle's home in the country for a happy Christmas holiday.

Their home had been my home too, for many years, and I was always pleased to return. Unfortunately, there was foot-and-mouth disease in their village that Christmas, and travel there was forbidden. However, my good uncle had managed to arrange a special pass, so as the bus travelled the last few kilometres through the restricted zone, I was the only passenger. I was driven straight to my uncle's gate.

"Here she is – our future foreigner," I heard the familiar voices say in welcome. What bliss! The countryside looked beautiful, and the house was cleaned and decorated to perfection for Christmas, so it glowed with welcoming warmth.

The snow was plentiful that year. At midday, just for a while, the snow-clad fields and trees glittered in the uncertain sunshine, and in the evening twilight it all looked majestically blue. The silence was so absolute, you could almost touch it. I could even hear my own heart beat while I was skiing with my little cousin across the thick ice on the softly snow-covered lake.

On Christmas Eve, the delicious smell of cooking filled the kitchen and gave promise of our traditional Christmas dinner – fish, and a whole ham boiled and then baked in the oven with various vegetable pies.

After a light lunch, the tall Christmas tree was brought in and everybody helped decorate it with flags, ribbons, coloured balls, real candles and a large shiny silver star at the top. The sauna stove had been lit and the presents were wrapped and hidden away in the hall cupboard.

My uncle had invited the two local policemen for a sauna and dinner – they were guarding the road outside, because of the travel restrictions. They were the first to go into the sauna, with its fierce heat that the men enjoyed so much. Then my aunt and her only son Ari went, followed lastly by my grandmother and me.

5

With my arm in hers, I carefully guided my grandmother along the snowy garden path, in the twilight, to the sauna. There was a hard frost but no wind. The silence was total. The dark blue dusk seemed to merge with the sky and cover everything – the garden, trees and even the sauna – with its shimmering magic.

Suddenly, I heard tinkling bells and saw a horse and sledge moving as if it were gliding through the blue twilight, leaving an echo of chiming bells.

"It must be Father Christmas," I said to my grandmother.

"Well, he has to start early. He doesn't leave any houses unvisited nowadays, like he used to when I was young," she said.

The sauna was still enjoyably hot, and from its dry heat I ran into the deep snow, rolling in it and covering myself, before standing there in the cold, steaming and cooling off. I'm sure I heard those tinkling bells again – a heavenly sound in the silence of the blue evening.

I washed my grandmother's back, and she did mine, and after a couple more minutes in the sauna's last heat, we walked arm in arm, wrapped in the warmth of our clothes and our love, back to the house. In the distance, beyond the garden and across the road, I could see a few village houses with their windows lit up, radiating Christmas warmth and welcome.

While we were dressing, I could hear my uncle busying himself with bottles of drink. The cocktails were ready – well tested and tasted, I judged from my uncle's jovial face. Even the policemen accepted a drink at Christmas, to lift their spirits.

After a long and enjoyable dinner, we savoured precious coffee and liquor, both saved especially for this evening. Then we realised that the most important event, at least for little Ari, was still missing. He kept asking if

Father Christmas had missed our house altogether, or if the reindeer had caught foot and mouth.

But no – at last we heard the sound of the reindeer's tinkling bells outside. Then came a heavy foot on the step, followed by a loud knock on the door.

"It's him!" exclaimed Ari, jumping up and looking anxiously at us all. I went to open the door, while Ari gathered his courage at his father's side.

"Good evening. Come in Father Christmas," said my uncle. "You look tired from visiting so many houses. Would you like a drink?" We all greeted this white-bearded old man, dressed in a fur coat and boots, and with a red, fur-lined hat.

"Yes, I would love one," said Father Christmas. "This sack is so heavy." Then, catching Ari's eye, he said, "I believe there are some good children in this house."

There was talk about travelling by reindeer in the restricted zone, but at last the high point of the evening came for Ari – the presents. But before he was given any, he had to recite a poem for Father Christmas.

Surprisingly, there were a lot of gifts – mostly useful things now that more shops were able to fill their shelves. One of my parcels contained a bra – a typical war-time present. Not knowing what was inside, I opened it quickly, then closed it just as fast but not before the not-so-old Father Christmas had spotted it and declared that he was allowed to give it to me only if we tried it to see if it was the right size!

Gradually, Ari's eyes began to close, and he went up to bed, taking his favourite presents with him. Father Christmas had one for the road, and we had our nightcap. So ended a perfect Christmas.

Back in Helsinki, I had a little farewell party for my friends. How they teased me about going to such a foggy, smoggy, dirty country with its cold bedrooms.

But I was prepared. I had made myself large pyjamas from the thickest flannelette I could find. I would be able to stay warm inside the long trousers and extra-long sleeves. My friends insisted that I show them my pyjamas. After their laughter and teasing, I told them, emphatically, that I was going only for a year and not a day longer.

Some of my friends took me to the station. The farewells were sad and drawn out because I was going so far away.

I was going to England.

Chapter 2

The first leg of the journey took me to Pori, where the captain met me at the station and took me to his ship. He told me that they were still loading timber but we should soon be ready to sail. It was very cold, and there was even more snow at Pori than there was in Helsinki. The sea was covered in thick ice.

The ship was new and warm, and my cabin with its bunk bed was very comfortable, even luxurious. I was the only passenger and the captain took me on a tour of the ship. I spent the rest of the day getting to know it, without disturbing anyone. Dinner that evening was delicious, but was over quickly.

Apparently, we were ahead of time and planned to leave with other ships in the middle of the night. All of us were to follow an icebreaker. The wind had packed the previously frozen ice up against the harbour, leaving iced mush nine metres thick. The icebreaker, with its strong lights, was leading the convoy.

It slowly started to advance, heaving the ice up and down around us and making a thunderous roar in the darkness. I spent most of that night on the bridge, watching the water and ice gurgling behind the ship that was immediately in front of us. By the first light of the morning, the ice had thinned, and soon the icebreaker left us in the clear waters of the Baltic Sea.

It seemed to me like an arctic expedition in that white world, and now we had the cold black sea in front of us, with a dark, heavy sky hanging above. Luckily, there was no wind until the afternoon, when the heavy sky delivered a snowstorm that followed us for the rest of the day.

The four-day trip went by pleasantly and lazily for me. I filled the time reading, walking the decks, and visiting the bridge to study the charts.

In the evenings, I listened to the captain and officers as they talked about their voyages to distant and strange lands.

It was morning when we approached the Thames estuary; by the afternoon, we had moored at Surrey Docks. It was January 1953, and I could hardly believe that at last I was in London, England.

From the ship, I had been watching the villages and suburbs getting larger and more tightly packed with houses. Now I was there among them, in the East End of London. My decision had become reality.

Customs officers came aboard to inspect the ship, and then unloading could begin. I was daydreaming on the bridge, when the captain brought me to my senses. "You must come and see the unloading," he said. "You'll see that all dockers here are gentlemen; they all wear ties." It was true. I saw only one docker without a tie.

Next morning, the captain took me with him by taxi to the City to visit the banks, shipping and insurance agents, and finally to a restaurant to have lunch of roast lamb and mint sauce.

"This mint sauce is new to me. It's delicious," I said. "And who says the English have no national dress? I've seen lots of them in the City, with dark suits and bowler hats – and even better, in tail coats with top hats!"

The captain told me he had another treat in store for me. He was taking me to see a show at the Prince of Wales Theatre, Piccadilly Circus. I could only sigh and say that I had read so much about Piccadilly Circus and couldn't wait to see it.

That night, Piccadilly Circus was a magical place to me. It was like fairyland, with lights flickering all around me. The show was funny and spectacular, although to my annoyance I nearly always laughed in the wrong place. My confidence in the English language was badly shaken.

After a couple more days' sightseeing, including dining at the Café Royal, the captain rang Mrs Dixon to tell her that I would be travelling to Birmingham by train and would be wearing a long brown fur coat with a long green silk scarf. Her chauffeur, Mr Knight, would be sent to meet me at the station, I was told.

The captain took me to the correct station in London and got a porter to take my cases to the train. Shaking my hand, he wished me luck, and added: "I'll see you in a year's time, and by then we'll speak only English."

I thanked him for all his help and kindness, and said I wondered how long it would be before I saw another Finn. He reassured me by saying that I was bound to meet some Finns in Birmingham, but advised me to forget them and my Finnish. "You're here to become an English lady and you have only a year to do it," he said.

The train moved slowly out of the station, leaving behind my only link with home. I was alone with my thoughts; there was so much to think about. But my mind was soon occupied as I watched the tall, smoke-blackened old terraced houses with their shabby little gardens.

Then my thoughts ran ahead of me, to the house where I was going. I wondered if it was anything like the bigger ones I'd passed in the outer suburbs of London. I wondered if Mrs Dixon would turn out to be like the two elderly ladies sharing my train compartment.

How was I going to cope with the English language? Would I even be able to understand Mrs Dixon? For practice, I tried to listen to the two elderly ladies, and became more and more worried when I realised I could understand only a few words.

In the Helsinki Finnish British Society, I could understand English and even speak it. But then most of us were Finns and it's always easier to understand foreigners speaking it. They try so hard to say it correctly, pronouncing every word separately and carefully.

11

It was too late to worry about it now. I had to learn it, and what better opportunity? I relaxed a little, so I could enjoy the beautiful English countryside as it flew past. It was so wonderfully green, even in the winter. My friends in Finland would be astonished to hear about it, I thought.

After passing through a couple of industrial towns, we approached the centre of Birmingham. When the train pulled in, I got off and stood on the platform with my cases, hoping that Mr Knight would see me. He must have been shown my photograph and told what coat I would be wearing.

At last, I spotted a man wearing a peaked cap, who looked as lost as I felt. He carried a piece of paper in his hand. He saw me and, after a quick glance at the piece of paper, he started to move slowly towards me. A faint smile appeared on his red face.

"Are you Miss Kaisu?" he asked. I understood only that he was saying my name, and how strange even that sounded here. "Yes," I managed to say, and he asked me to follow him. He took my cases, while I picked up the rest of my luggage and followed this small plump man, who was wearing a dark raincoat. He turned around once to see if I was following, and I noticed the letters PTL on his cap.

The black and square-looking Ford 8 car was parked quite near. We packed the cases in and I went to sit next to them on the back seat. Mr Knight climbed into the driver's seat, then turned round, smiled, and said: "It's not very far to go – just in Moseley," and turned on the engine to drive me to my new home.

He said something more about Moseley, and I also heard the word Tennessee, but I couldn't understand what he was saying so I gathered my courage and asked: "What does PTL mean?"

Mr Knight stretched his neck round and replied "Pocket Testament League".

"Really? What is that?" I asked. I couldn't understand much of his answer, so I concentrated on looking out at the wonders of Birmingham.

First there was the busy centre of the city, with all its shops, and then came long rows of houses, just like the ones I'd seen in the picture book of industrial Britain, back in Finland.

Further out, there were bigger houses, with lush gardens even in January. We turned into a quiet avenue of trees and large houses. "Moor Green Lane," Mr Knight announced. I remembered the address. So this was the street where the house called Tennessee was located.

I straightened up in my seat, and looked around anxiously to see which house it was going to be. Mr Knight slowed down and drove through an open gate. There were two nameplates on the gatepost: one said "Tennessee" and the other said "in".

The driveway was concealed from the road by a low wall and a thick hedge; it led round in a curve in front of the house, and back out to the street by another gate. On the garden side of the hedge was a lawn, and it was full of snowdrops.

The car stopped outside the heavy oak front door studded with nails. I stepped out and looked at the large red-brick house. Among a few small windows, I noticed two large ones, which made it look less like a prison, I thought.

We lifted the cases onto the front step. My heart was racing with anxiety and fear, as I stood next to Mr Knight in front of that large, nailed door. He rang the bell and, after what seemed an eternity, the door slowly creaked open.

In the doorway stood a small and very thin middle-aged woman. Her hair was dark and pulled back tightly, and her pallid face made her look ill. Her dark blue shapeless dress hung from her thin shoulders and reached almost to her ankles.

13

Mr Knight said something to her, and she turned to me and smiled. I smiled back and said, "I am Kaisu. Greetings from Finland," just as I had practised in the train.

She replied, "How do you do? I'm Miss Brown, the secretary. Welcome to Tennessee. Now let's go upstairs and see Mrs Dixon, shall we?"

To my surprise, I could understand her well, and her kind smile helped me to relax. We carried the suitcases into the dark hall, and the door closed behind me. Miss Brown smiled again and said, "I hope you had a good journey. Mrs Dixon is waiting for you in her study." Her voice was quiet and kind.

"Yes thank you," I answered, and followed her, glancing at a massive Dutch cupboard on the way. We passed a large glass case full of stuffed seagulls, which divided the hall. Behind it were armchairs, beautiful paintings and a handsome grandfather clock.

On the right side was a wide staircase. On reaching the half landing, I saw one of the large windows that I'd noticed when I arrived. It was prominent and impressive, and with its stained glass it could have been a church window if it weren't for the red velvet curtains hanging at the sides.

Once on the first floor landing, Miss Brown quietly opened a door, put her head inside, and I heard her say, "Mrs Dixon, Kaisu has arrived."

She turned and gently pushed me into the room in front of her.

Chapter 3

My employer stood in the middle of the room. She was wearing a blue dress that matched the colour of the carpet, and was leaning on a stick. Her soft, curly white hair was pinned up on top of her head. She must have been beautiful when she was young, I thought, and she still had dignity of presence. Her smile was welcoming and her bright blue eyes seemed to be smiling, too.

I walked towards her.

"Ah, here you are at last, Kaisu," she greeted me. She let her stick drop while she hugged me as if I were her long-lost child.

"Greetings from Finland," I replied. "I am so glad to be here after a long journey."

They were the words I had practised so carefully. She hugged me again, against her ample bosom, and her pink, downy cheek felt soft on my own.

Then she pushed me from her, still with her hand on my shoulder to steady herself without her stick, and she looked at me searchingly.

"Did you have a good journey?" she asked, speaking slowly through her false teeth. We remained standing while I told her about my journey.

"Thank you also for giving me the chance to brush up on my English," I said to her. "It is the most important language in the world."

"It is indeed," she answered, "at least in the western world."

Finally, she asked Miss Brown to take me to meet Frieda, the German au pair, who would help me carry my cases upstairs. I again followed Miss Brown along the landing, this time to the servants' staircase and down to the servants' sitting room, where Frieda was reading.

She jumped up as we came into the room, and we shook hands.

"Hello Kaisu," she said. "How nice that you've come here. I've been lonely by myself."

I told her that I was glad she was there to keep me company.

Miss Brown went out, closing the door behind her, saying she'd leave us to get to know each other. But despite her instant friendliness, Frieda seemed shy once we were on our own. She was bigger than me, but with a slightly rounded back, and she didn't look very strong. Her short and very dark hair framed a nice round face. Her eyes were dark blue, her cheeks very red, and the right one had a sweet dimple.

"Shall we take your cases up first, and then have some tea?" she asked.

"Yes," I said, "and perhaps you can tell me all about this place."

I was just beginning to take in the dark brown room. It had brown walls and a carpet that had probably had a pattern decades before. There was a dark brown Welsh dresser but it was empty except for a couple of books and an empty vase. There was a brown table and brown chairs. Even the two small armchairs either side of the fireplace were brown. There was only one brightly-coloured item in the whole room: it was a beaded lampshade that reminded me of one in my grandmother's house.

"This is our sitting room," said Frieda. She pointed to a small table on which there was an old wooden radio with decorative carving in front of the speaker. "We're lucky; we have the only radio in the house," she said. "It's old but somehow it works."

As we went through the door with my cases, Frieda pointed out the kitchen, the dining room, and the butler's pantry, and led me up the staircase to the big hall where my cases were standing. Frieda said she'd show me round the house after tea. I commented on how grand and old everything looked.

"It's a bit like a museum but you'll get used to it," said Frieda.

We picked up the cases and retraced our steps to the servants' staircase. It was so narrow and twisting, that I could only just heave my cases up behind Frieda.

At last we reached the second floor. "This is our territory," said Frieda, "apart from Miss Brown's study at the end of the corridor." She opened a door and stepped into a room. "This is your room, next to the bathroom," she told me.

Apprehensively, I stepped inside. I stood there for a long time, with my suitcase in my hand. So this was the end of my journey to my dream – my home for a whole year.

I looked at the white-painted iron bed, which seemed to be sinking in the middle.

"This room is all right, Frieda, but not exactly cosy. I do hope yours is better," I said.

"Yes, mine is cosier because it's smaller," she said.

I put my suitcase by the small wardrobe that stood against the long wall. On the other side of the room was a gas fire, with a small armchair in front of it. By the window was a table and a chair, and in the middle of the lino-covered floor was a small, faded carpet. Seeing the expression on my face, Frieda said she thought the house hadn't been decorated for several decades.

Opening the wardrobe, I found four wooden coathangers.

"I nearly brought some with me," I said, taking one out and showing it to Frieda.

"I know where I can find a couple more for you," Frieda said, as if she'd located a gold mine. "Come to see my room first, and then we can go down for tea."

Her room was indeed cosier, and from her high window – if you stood on a chair to look out – there was a lovely view over the garden. The last rays of the winter sun made the room look more cheerful.

17

"Let's go," said Frieda, leading me out and closing the door. "I must look after Mrs Dixon."

I followed her down the stairs to the kitchen.

Like everything else in the house, the kitchen was much bigger than I'd imagined. In the middle, on the red-tiled floor, was an enormous wooden table that had been scrubbed clean and white. On one long wall was a Welsh dresser with silver-plated meat dishes and covers on the shelves.

Under the window, which opened onto a glassed-in kitchen terrace, was a big, deep and well-worn porcelain double sink. It had wooden draining boards on either side, and instead of a cupboard underneath, there was just a bucket and a wooden platform to stand on. I knew I'd need that platform to be able to reach the bottom of the sink.

As the only concession to modernisation, the coal-fired cooking range had been removed, and in its place were two grey gas cookers, one each side of the chimneypiece. They looked as if they were the first ones ever made.

In the corner was a door to the outside, and along the nearby wall were a couple of chairs and a door leading down to the cellar.

"Mrs Dixon keeps her eggs down there," said Frieda, as she filled two pots of tea; one for Mrs Dixon and one for us.

"Mrs Dixon and Miss Brown have thinly-cut bread and butter with jam," she told me. "Their biscuits are kept upstairs."

The tray was ready, and Frieda said she'd take it to the nursery.

"To the nursery?" I asked. "I didn't think she had any children."

"No she hasn't," Frieda said, from the doorway. "But the nursery is still there, even with all its toys."

Feeling sad for Mrs Dixon, I took our tray to our sitting room.

"As you see," said Frieda, as she joined me, "we have rock cakes today in your honour."

"What a nice thought," I said. "This is my first English tea in an English house, and it tastes very good."

There were a thousand questions I wanted to ask about the house and its people, but first I needed to get to know Frieda.

"I was with another family before coming here," she began, "but I can tell you that this is the best house you can be in in England. We have so little to do, there's lots of time left for studying.

"In Germany, I studied English for years before coming here. Now I go to town once a week, to an English class. The teacher is very good and we meet up with our friends there."

I asked if I could join her, and she quickly agreed.

"Mrs Dixon doesn't give us a day off," Frieda went on, "but up to now I haven't missed it. She is very good about giving us free time in the afternoons, as long as it doesn't disturb her routine. But free time outside the house and garden is very limited."

Although Frieda was rather shy, there was determination and purpose in her voice.

"We girls are like Mrs Dixon's captives," she told me. "We're her safety valve against loneliness. She wants us here all the time and treats us as if we were her own children. But we are only au pair girls, and for the sake of learning English and £2 a week, we stay with her."

As I heard this, I thought, with disappointment, of the year ahead.

Frieda went on to explain the routine of the house.

"First thing in the morning, we have to make tea for the postman. He comes soon after 7am. Mrs Dixon has her tea in bed, at 8 o'clock, and soon afterwards Mrs Allen comes in to make our breakfast. When that's finished and the dishes washed up, we clean and dust the house with her. Mrs Allen leaves by midday.

"Mrs Meyer then arrives to make our lunch. Of course, we do the vegetables and the washing up. We make the tea, too, and supper is only bread and cheese with a cup of cocoa."

This didn't sound at all bad to me.

"What about the laundry?" I asked.

"We wash our own smalls," Frieda told me, "and the rest Mrs Dixon sends away for cleaning. The enormous laundry room behind the kitchen is redundant."

After we'd had tea, Frieda took me to the nursery to collect the tray. Mrs Dixon and Miss Brown were still sitting at the table, where there were some important-looking papers. Mrs Dixon noticed me, and said: "Ah Kaisu. Did I say your name correctly? You must tell me what it means, because it sounds Japanese to me."

Turning to Miss Brown, she said, "We used to have good friends, Japanese missionaries. Do you remember them? They came here a couple of years ago. Their name was Kiso."

Turning back to me, she again asked if she'd pronounced my name correctly.

"Yes, perfectly," I told her, encouragingly. "Your other name is Marjatta, isn't it?" she asked. "What does Kaisu mean?"

I told her that Kaisu was the same as Katherine, and that there were many versions of the name in Finland. Frieda and Miss Brown could see that this was going to be a lengthy discussion, and they quietly left the room. They were right – it did take a long time, as I told Mrs Dixon about my family and other relations. She was quite fascinated by my surname, Hurri, which for some 400 years has been the name of the farm and estate where my father was born and which is still in the family.

"So sad about your family," said Mrs Dixon, after I told her how they had been killed in the war. "We have to trust in God's way in this. But I am now your English mother and I will take good care of you and Frieda," she assured me.

"Thank you," I replied. "I'm sure I'll be very happy here," adding silently to myself, "come what may."

"Come now," said Mrs Dixon. "I want to show you the house. Miss Brown will be busy in her office, won't you Miss Brown?"

It was only when she turned around to talk to Miss Brown that she realised she'd already left the room.

Leaning on the table, she slowly stood up and found her stick behind her. I noticed that her left leg was shorter than her right, and that she had a thick-soled lace-up shoe on it. Later, I heard many times about the car accident that had caused her disability.

"The room we're in is the nursery," Mrs Dixon told me. "I have my breakfast and tea here. The morning sun is very pleasant in this room." It was a big room, and aside from the large table in the centre, it was packed full with all kinds of chairs, bookshelves, cupboards and a small settee.

From there, I followed her to the nanny's room, nursemaid's room and the playroom. This was like a glassed-in balcony, with bright green painted woodwork around the windows. It was full of toys, including a dolls' house, a cradle full of dolls, and a beautiful rocking horse.

"Some of these were my own toys. I used to play with them," Mrs Dixon told me with a big smile and a little laugh. She seemed happy with her memories, but I thought she was trying to hide her loneliness.

"These dolls are beautiful – so beautiful," I said, "and the dolls' house is so big and fully furnished. It's a treasure. I wish I was a little girl in this wonderland."

Mrs Dixon looked at me sadly and turned towards the door.

"Here is our linen room," she told me. "I do the laundry basket here myself each week. I think Frieda can show you the rest of the house, because I have work to do."

We never mentioned the playroom again, although I went there sometimes to look at the lovely old toys.

Chapter 4

Frieda didn't show me around the house that evening. "We'll leave it until the morning when we'll be doing the dusting tour with Mrs Allen," she said. "Let's just talk and have our supper this evening."

I agreed, and asked to hear Mrs Dixon's story. Frieda told me all she knew, saying that Mrs Dixon herself would fill in all the gaps.

"She loves talking about her husbands, especially the first one – 'Dear Mr Alexander' as she calls him," Frieda said.

I learned that Mrs Dixon was the second-youngest child of an important industrialist. Her grandfather, John Cadbury, and his brother Benjamin had started a chocolate-making business that was later taken over by John's two sons Richard and Simon.

Being Quakers and Puritans, they were naturally against the evils of the world, and drunkenness was one of them, so cocoa was launched as the ideal substitute for alcohol. The strongly active temperance movement gave the new firm its blessing, and the Cadbury name became a household word and made the family very rich.

Behind Tennessee's four-acre garden, and across the road, was the old family home. It was a grand building in vast grounds and was now a school for handicapped children.

Mr Alexander had been an American evangelist from Tennessee, Texas – hence the name of the house. He was the Billy Graham of the Victorian and Edwardian era, travelling around the world spreading the gospel and preaching his beliefs.

He had come to Birmingham at the beginning of the century, to hold a meeting at Bingley Hall. Mrs Dixon's family was there; Mr Alexander and Helen met, and in three months they were engaged to be married. For 17 years, until his death, the marriage was blissfully happy, despite the couple's sadness at having no children.

They built this wonderful house and garden and had many servants. They travelled together all over the world, on missionary work, and made many friends who often came to visit them in later years. Mrs Dixon often told us stories about their exciting years together. Sometimes, the tales were very confused, and at other times she became stuck on the smallest details. She was always very proud of the fact that she had been a sporty girl, and a good car driver.

"Our family had one of the first American cars in England," she told us, once. "I was a jolly good driver in those days and very daring. That was when the accident happened. Now I have a short leg because I had to have a big operation."

We heard Mrs Dixon coming to the servants' hall, her heavy shoe and stick sounding on the tiled floor. "She's going to wash her eggs," Frieda told me. "You must be very tired. I'll clear these dishes away so you can go to bed. We'll take it in turns after that. Let's go and say goodnight to Mrs Dixon."

We carried our supper plates to the kitchen, where Mrs Dixon was starting her evening work.

"Art thou not tired yet, Kaisu?" she asked when she saw me. "Thou will sleep sweetly tonight, with God's blessing." She often used the archaic personal pronoun, as was the old Quaker custom.

She noticed that I had been looking at the eggs. "These are my bantam eggs," she explained. "They are delicious. Villis, our gardener, keeps the bantams and brings the eggs here every evening. I wash them myself and take them down to the cellar. Thou must come and see them."

She took my hand and, opening a door, led me down some rickety-looking steps.

"Be careful now," she advised. "Thou mustn't get hurt on thy first day here."

She told me all about her eggs – how she washed them with vinegar, counted them, kept a book about their numbers, and finally put them on trays in the dusty and otherwise empty cellar.

After what seemed a long lecture, we struggled back up the rickety steps. I was afraid that I might find her dead one day, or immobile on top of her bantam eggs.

Frieda had done the dishes and was waiting for us.

"Frieda and Kaisu, my dear, dear children. You ought to go to bed now. Tomorrow will be a strenuous day for dear Kaisu," said Mrs Dixon.

"Don't forget our postman in the morning. Goodnight my darling German Frieda, and goodnight my little blonde Finn Kaisu."

She laughed, hugged us and kissed us on the cheek.

"Goodnight and sleep well," we replied as we left the kitchen.

As Frieda and I climbed the stairs to the second floor, she whispered to me, "It'll be hours before Mrs Dixon goes to bed – usually after 1 o'clock in the morning. I always hear her when I'm reading in bed."

"What does she do?" I asked.

"Heaven knows," replied Frieda. "She walks and does everything at a snail's pace. Everything takes hours for her."

I remarked, "She is living according to Parkinson's Law – her work fills her day. At least she has no time to get bored."

As Frieda and I parted on the landing, I asked her to wake me up in the morning so I didn't oversleep. My own room was as cold as charity. There was a box of matches on the mantelshelf, so I lit the gas fire as I had seen Frieda doing in our sitting room. Unpacking my cases, I put my new pyjamas on the chair to warm up by the fire. Soon I was in my own cold bed.

I found that the light switch was by the door, so I had to get up again. The day's events went round in my head for a few minutes, until I fell into a dreamless sleep.

Next morning, I heard Frieda's knock on my door. Jumping up from my bed, I suddenly realised that I wasn't in Finland, I wasn't on board ship at sea – I was getting out of that sagging iron bed in England.

The cold bedroom and the sense of duty shocked me into action. I managed to light the fire and warm my clothes in front of it for a moment, before putting them on.

How simple my life had become. Although I was now in my late 20s, I needed only to comb my hair – no make-up, no nail varnish, and no fancy clothes any more. Thank goodness I had prepared on the train – all my mascara and lipstick had been wiped off and stowed away for a year. Oh well, I thought, life could only get better after this year.

Our morning went slowly. I dutifully followed Frieda everywhere – when she took the cup of tea with two biscuits to the postman, and later the same to Mrs Dixon's bedside.

Soon after, Mrs Allen stomped in, puffing and blowing, and slumped down into a kitchen chair. No wonder she's like that, I thought, carrying all that bosom and weight, but her rosy cheeks were creased in a smile at me, and her eyes twinkled.

Frieda had told me that Mrs Allen was only fat, not old. She was about 40, married to a council worker, and had two daughters.

She burst out with, "So you're Kaisu! Hello and welcome. Had a nice journey?"

Before I could answer, she carried on, "You'll like it here. It's not hard and difficult and we have some good laughs at times. Hope you like bacon and egg. We have it every morning."

"Yes, I love it," I managed to say, before she started again.

"So glad you've come here," she said, almost without pausing for breath. "Poor Frieda must have been so lonely. Talking about loneliness, you should have seen this comedian on television last night. He was really funny. How many slices of bacon for you, Kaisu? What a funny name you have. So foreign."

Soon the smell of cooking bacon – now the most gorgeous smell in the world – filled the kitchen. We three had our breakfast in the sitting room, and then Mrs Allen hurried back to the kitchen to cook the bacon and bantams' eggs for Mrs Dixon.

"Have you ever tried these bantam eggs?" I asked Frieda.

"No chance. They're too well counted," she said.

She took the tray up to Mrs Dixon, while I cleared our sitting room and washed up the dishes.

"When shall we start the serious business of dusting the house?" I asked, impatiently.

"Cheeky!" responded Mrs Allen, with a twinkle in her eyes, as she went to fetch the dusters.

Frieda and I were like two pageboys following a duchess, with a duster in one hand and a bottle of polish in the other. "We always start with the bedroom and study, while Mrs Dixon is having her breakfast," explained Mrs Allen, leading the way up the grand staircase.

I'd been in the study the day before, but had been concentrating too much on my English and Mrs Dixon to notice much else. Now I saw Dear Mr Alexander in a life-sized photograph beside the door. He was a jolly-looking, smiling man in a waistcoat and striped trousers, a bowler hat and a walking stick.

"Lucky man – he is still in this house like a guardian angel and greatly loved," I said, without thinking. "He must have been good like 'dear Albert'," I continued, then realised what I'd said, and blushed.

Years earlier, a Finnish girlfriend had told me that 'dear Albert', Queen Victoria's husband, had been given his fine monument in Hyde Park, London, because he was so good in bed.

"Naughty, aren't we?" said Mrs Allen, realising my meaning.

Just a few weeks later, while dusting in the bedroom, she told us to open the top drawer of the bedside table. As Frieda slowly opened the drawer, Mrs Allen told her, "Look to the left. There's a piece of glass."

Frieda held up a smooth piece of greenish-coloured matt glass, rather like a straight banana.

"What is it?" we chorused.

"You don't know?" replied Mrs Allen, disbelievingly. "Guess!"

We both insisted we had no idea. By now, Mrs Allen was obviously embarrassed, and tried to delay answering us. At last, she said, "Mrs Dixon must have used this after she became a widow."

"No! I don't believe it," we again chorused.

The incident made me think that Mrs Dixon must have been very lonely at times. The happy married life she'd enjoyed was reflected and captured in the dozens of photographs around the house. Frieda told me that Mrs Dixon had been married a second time, to a much older man – a Mr Dixon, who was a doctor of divinity – but he'd died soon afterwards. There was a large picture of him in the hall.

The study was a pleasant, light room, with a pale blue carpet, small blue armchairs, and little tables. There were dozens of pictures and photographs on the mantelshelf, tables and walls. By the window stood a large roll-top desk.

We learned to make Mrs Dixon's bed in a special way – it involved plumping up the pillows and covering up the box at the foot of the bed that kept the weight of the bedclothes off Mrs Dixon's feet.

After dusting all the many knickknacks in her bedroom, we cleaned the toilet and bathroom. I was surprised to see how spartan the bathroom was, especially as it was the only one in the house, apart from our own which was much nicer and had a double hand basin. Mrs Dixon's was just functional, and impossible to luxuriate in. But then that would have been a sinful thing to do.

After that, we had to dust and look over the three spacious guest bedrooms. On the landing, Mrs Allen opened the doors of a grand mahogany wardrobe. The moths seemed to love this dark, quiet place, which was full of Mrs Dixon's old dresses. One day, she took them all out and told me the story of each one.

On the way downstairs to our elevenses, we lovingly polished Dear Mr Alexander's gramophone with its beautiful brass horn.

"All his hymns are on records in this cupboard underneath," Mrs Allen told us.

"Really?" I said, excitedly. "I'd love to play them some time. Do you think we could ask Mrs Dixon?"

"Well, you can, but I wouldn't," said Mrs Allen, on her way to our sitting room.

As we followed her, I whispered to Frieda, "We'll play them before we leave this place."

Elevenses was a new experience for me. Here, below stairs, we had the chicory-tasting coffee called Camp, with biscuits, while Mrs Allen took a thermos flask of hot water to Mrs Dixon so she could make Nescafé coffee.

I never really got used to Camp Coffee because, in Finland, we would pay anything for our one luxury of good coffee. I'd been spoiled like this, but thank goodness I

29

wasn't choosy about my food. In fact, I've yet to find any food, provided that it's well prepared, that I can't eat.

"Drink up, girls," said Mrs Allen. "We still have downstairs to do."

We followed her to the drawing room in which the prominent item was the grand piano. Otherwise, the furniture wasn't heavy and the two south-facing windows, with faded pink velvet curtains, made it a cheerful room.

The dining room was just the opposite. The walls were covered in real red velvet, cut to a renaissance pattern and looked very Victorian. The dining chairs were covered with the same material; there must have been nearly 20 of them, all lined up against one wall, opposite a carved fireplace. The oak table in the middle of the room was massive, and its carved legs were shapely and thick.

The high sideboard matched the table, but was more ornately carved. The poor Turkish-patterned carpet had obviously seen better days, and was dangerous for Mrs Dixon's unsteady walk. Much later, the carpet was replaced by a very similar one. At that time, Mrs Dixon said to me with a chuckle, looking at the newer carpet, "My child, I found it. Can you believe it? I found it in the storeroom, still wrapped up in newspapers. What's more, I remember the day when I was 17 and went to London with my mother and we bought this carpet."

"But that was 60 years ago," I exclaimed, in amazement.

"Yes my dear, and so are the newspapers. It's perfect for this room. Even the pattern matches the walls, and the red and blue colours are still superb."

I wanted to ask her if she still remembered the price, but as money was never discussed in this house, I didn't say anything.

Chapter 5

No sooner had Mrs Allen left for the day, than Mrs Meyer appeared, with her shopping basket full of ingredients for our lunch, which she dumped on the table.

She was a petite and spry person, and although ordinarily dressed, she had a certain intellectual but friendly bearing. She was a cookery teacher by profession. Her husband was also a teacher, and their son, who was in his last year at university, was to become a teacher too. They were Austrian, but had been living in England for some years. Their daughter was married and lived in Vienna.

I liked Mrs Meyer straight away. Her English was perfect, and so unlike Mrs Allen's accent, which for a long while I could hardly understand – even though she spoke very loudly to us.

Mrs Meyer was easier and more interesting to listen to. From the very first day, and even more later on when I'd lost my shyness, she and we girls talked about all sorts of things. She was the source of all information about events in the world and our town.

Mrs Meyer greeted me with, "Hello Kaisu. We've been waiting for you so eagerly. This house is too big for just two people in it all night." She added, "You'll be glad to know that Mrs Dixon really needs you here. I hope I'll hear all about your journey during lunch, but first I must cook it."

Her lunches were our daily surprise, although sometimes we were asked what we'd like for the next one. Frieda usually asked to have sauerkraut and frankfurters, while my own choice was salmon and new potatoes – both unfulfilled hopes!

This time, we had pork chops with apple sauce, potatoes and cabbage, followed by apple pie and custard. We girls did the vegetables and laid the tables – one table for us, in our sitting room, and a small table by the window

in the dining room for Mrs Dixon. We had to light a candle
for her, and place it in the plate-warmer by her table – it
was necessary for her because her lunch took her so long to
eat.

Everything was ready now, so Frieda went to the hall
outside the butler's pantry, where an important instrument
was standing on its bamboo legs – a xylophone – to call
Mrs Dixon to lunch.

I didn't realise what Frieda was playing, and next day
when I asked to play the lunch bell, I did it so badly that it
brought Mrs Dixon down straight away. There and then,
she taught me the right tune. It was the chime of Big Ben,
before the time signal on the radio, which I hadn't yet
heard. It had to be played three times running, loud and
clear, so that Mrs Dixon could hear it in any room in the
large house.

We enjoyed our lunch and talk, and I was already
looking forward to the next day. Mrs Meyer had brought us
the previous day's newspaper.

"You must read it," she said. "You will realise that
journalists' language isn't perfect. When you read it and
listen to the radio, you'll understand the spoken language
much better."

It was so true. At times, I really worried that I wouldn't
be able to understand anything on the radio. It always
sounded like a string of words without any sense or
separation between them. Sometimes, I had to put my ear
so close to the radio that I was touching it, but the words
were still too fast for me. However, slowly I became used
to the radio, and it was a very important teacher of perfect
English.

Once we had done the washing up after lunch, I told
Frieda that I'd like to see the garden.

"I'll come with you," she said. "I've not been there for
some days as the weather has been so horrid."

We wrapped our thick cardigans around us and walked out through the kitchen door.

"What are those two doors here?" I asked, on our way out.

"Come and look," replied Frieda. "It's the deserted laundry room."

Before me were the iron pots for boiling the whites, deep cemented sinks, corrugated washing boards, wooden tables, and a wooden platform for standing on.

"It looks like a Victorian workhouse," I said in amazement. "I've seen pictures of them."

Frieda walked to the other door and opened it.

"This is another wonder," she announced. "It's our larder. It's empty now, but tomorrow we'll have deliveries of half a pound of ham for our Sunday tea, and sausages for our Sunday lunch.

"Believe it or not, we have no refrigerator in the house. At least the marble shelves are cold at this time of year, and Mrs Meyer brings fresh food every day, but what happens in the summer we'll have to wait and see."

We walked along the hedge-lined driveway towards the old stables, which had now been converted into garages, and homes for the bantams and Villis the gardener. Behind them was a low brick building that was used as a tea room for the summer missionary meetings.

We met Villis there, and Frieda introduced us. He was a lean, middle-aged man with a long face and very blue eyes. He told me he came from Lithuania, and had been a prisoner-of-war in England but had stayed here.

"My family is still in Lithuania – alive, I hope," he said.

"It's a cruel life for some. I'm sorry," I said.

"I'm happy here," continued Villis, "and I love the garden. Madam is very good to me. She never comes to my room." He gave us a toothy smile.

"The garden looks beautiful," said Frieda.

"Four precious acres in the middle of Birmingham, and ours for a year," I said.

Villis thanked us for his lunch, and we left him with his cat.

Frieda told me that Villis had the same lunch as us. It was put on a plate, with a cover over it, and he collected it from the veranda, returning the empty plate to the same place when he'd finished.

"Often, we don't see him for days," Frieda told me.

"He must be fed up with bantam egg omelettes for supper," I commented.

We walked towards the pond, where geese were chasing each other around the haystacks and back into the water.

"The haystacks are only here for show," Frieda told me. "They make Mrs Dixon imagine that she's living in the country."

There were more delights to come. We found a sunken garden, with rocks and alpine plants, and a deep lily pond in the centre that was large enough to have several wooden benches around it. On one side of the garden was a summerhouse, with a small covered terrace. It looked an ideal place to escape and read a book, I thought.

There were paths leading to secret corners behind the bushes and trees. At the back of the house was a large and well-kept lawn, with rose beds next to the building itself.

From the garden, the house looked so different – much cosier and more friendly. It was a Victorian house, although not opulently decorated. It looked as if every room had been designed separately, each with different styles and ideas, and then these "cubes" had somehow been fitted together to form the whole house.

I had always enjoyed looking at houses and buildings, ever since I was a child. I had wanted to be an architect, although I never achieved that ambition – the war intervened, and then nearly every Finnish man wanted to become an architect, so there wasn't much chance of a girl becoming one. But I still loved doodling building plans, and now, standing in this garden, I saw not just the outside of Tennessee but right through it.

While Frieda and I were having our tea, she told me more about the household.

"There are lots of people you haven't met yet," she said. "Tomorrow, you'll meet Dotty, and Mr Sedgewick the day after. They are real relics from olden times. Dotty is 80 years old and she still comes every week to polish the silver. Mr Sedgewick comes to wind the clocks."

"I'm really looking forward to meeting them," I said. "One isn't alone here for long, with so many people coming and going during the daytime."

"Yes, it's in the evenings that I realised I was alone, although I wasn't lonely," Frieda told me. "Thank goodness you're here now."

When I went to fetch Mrs Dixon's tray, she started to tell me about Dotty.

"She came to us as a little girl, to be a maid. She was so good and reliable that she became our parlour maid. Then I took her as a ladies maid. Now she's retired and lives with her sister in the village. You won't believe that she's 80 – she is wonderful," said Mrs Dixon.

She then proceeded to tell me, slowly and at great length, more about Dotty and about her other maids, all dead now.

Despite the bitterly cold weather, Dotty appeared next morning, wrapped in a long woollen scarf that covered her head and shoulders. She wore thick mittens and a long overcoat, but that wasn't long enough to cover her even longer blue dress and white apron.

I opened the door to her and saw her shivering, her wrinkle-free face purple with the cold. Her little eyes, behind now-steaming spectacles, were running with tears from the wind.

35

"Oh! You're the new girl here. I'm Dotty," she said.

"And I'm Kaisu," I responded.

"I'll come by the fire for a while," Dotty said, as she hurried to our sitting room.

Dotty was perfect. In her long dress and apron, she was definitely part of a past world. She didn't talk much, either – she just sipped her cup of hot tea.

"I'm so much warmer now," she told us, after her elevenses. "My sister and I don't go out much when it's very cold. She's much older than I am, and not as strong."

"You're fantastic for your age," we choroused, which pleased her.

We heard Mrs Dixon coming down the stairs, so Dotty, with her thick cardigan on, rushed off to the cold pantry to spread out the silver for polishing.

When I went in to see the silver, Mrs Dixon said affectionately, "This is my faithful Dotty. What would I do without her?" and she put an arm around Dotty's shoulders.

"What indeed?" I thought.

Mrs Dixon relied on Dotty and all her other helpers to do their jobs as they'd always been done, and without Mrs Dixon knowing how. I learned that if there was a crisis in the house, Dotty would be there to lend a hand. She wouldn't let her old employer down. She never complained but she continuously reminded us that she was 80 years old!

Another old soul in the house was Mr Sedgewick. He appeared each week, carrying long ladders from room to room to wind the clocks, more or less unnoticed. He hardly ever said a word. Once, at the end of my year, I spoke to him.

"Mr Sedgewick, you've been here every week as long as I've been here. Don't you ever take a holiday?"

"Yes Miss, every week. And do you know how long I've been coming here now?" he asked, proudly, his long grey moustache shaking with emotion.

"I've been here every week for more than 50 years. The clocks need me."

"I believe you," I said, "but you look so young. You must be fit to go up and down those ladders."

I saw a faint smile on his face, and heard a quiet "thank you, Miss."

Chapter 6

On Friday afternoon, when all was quiet except for the cold rain beating on the windows, I was alone in our sitting room, reading by the fire.

Suddenly, I heard someone moving in the kitchen. I went to investigate and found another old worker there, whom everyone had forgotten to mention to me. She was the charwoman, Mrs M, and she looked every inch a char, too, in her flowery loose dress and apron. She had a large, hanging bosom and her thin grey hair also hung, in a disarranged way over her red face. She was on her hands and knees, scrubbing the kitchen floor.

"Oh, sorry!" I said. "I didn't know anybody was here. I'm new in the house. I'm Kaisu."

"Yes, it's only me, Mrs M. Pleased to meet you," she said, as she staggered to her feet with difficulty. "I come here each week to clean the kitchen and the veranda," she told me.

I left her there, starting to scrub the kitchen table, and returned to my book beside the fire.

Later, I heard a noise coming from the hall, and went to see what it was. I found Mrs M there, cleaning the tiles to the hall terrace.

"It's you, Mrs M!" I said, in surprise, realising that I hadn't heard her walk past our sitting room, which meant she must have gone round the outside of the house.

"Why didn't you come here through the hall? It's raining heavily now, and you'll catch a cold in that thin dress."

To my greater surprise, she answered, "Oh no, Miss. I'm not allowed to come through the house. I've been charring here for over 25 years, but I've never been inside the house."

"Really?" I replied, in amazement. "Why not?"

"Well, it's not my place to go inside. I'm only the kitchen char," she said. "Mind you, I'm quite satisfied like this. It's all right. I just do this and then go home for my tea."

It was true – she wasn't offered even a cup of tea. I felt terribly sorry for her and her lowly status. Although I was very much in the same situation, I never felt inferior to any of the other people in the house, not even Mrs Dixon. I was born in a democratic country and lived in one of the most democratic societies in the world, and I was completely ignorant of any class system like this.

Many people in Finland, including some friends, had much more money than I did, but that was natural and one didn't need to feel ashamed. Perhaps, I thought, it was academic status that had created more inequality in my own country than bank balance or birth. Maybe, too, our equality was due to the good state schools in Finland, and not having had an industrial revolution; where the Prime Minister's son was likely to be the best friend of the dustman's son, knowing that their grandparents had come from the same independent farming class.

The farmers and small land-owners had been a great influence in Finland, as there were hardly any single owners of large areas of land, or landed gentry. They brought a sense of equality and democracy to society.

Here in England, I would have to learn the intricacies of the complicated British class system. But as a foreigner and a European, I was outside it. Mrs M was, of course, perfectly equal in her own class, but here she knew her place.

I was sad, because I thought that in this ultra-civilised country – here if anywhere – a person's pride would be respected. Now I realised that it was actually the opposite. Naturally, I had read about it but the reality was still a shock to me.

We could talk about social behaviour and the class system to Mrs Meyer. She was also an outsider, like Frieda and me, and from her independent viewpoint, we could learn a great deal.

Even Mrs Dixon considered Mrs Meyer as a near equal and talked to her with a greater respect than she did some of her other employees.

"She comes to help me out," Mrs Dixon would say about Mrs Meyer, despite the fact that Mrs Meyer had been doing the cooking at Tennessee for several years.

One day, when Mrs Allen and Mr Knight were talking in the kitchen, I heard Mrs Allen say, "Well I told Madam so."

Surprised, I said that I didn't know Mrs Dixon was referred to as "Madam".

"Of course," they chorused. "Don't you call her Madam?"

I said I called her Mrs Dixon, that I'd never called anyone Madam and didn't see why I should start now.

"Well you should," said Mrs Allen. "She's Madam to us, and that's the proper way to address her."

I thought to myself that if Mrs Dixon wanted to be our English mother, as she claimed, surely calling her Madam would have been very out of place in that sort of relationship.

Mrs Dixon greatly respected her secretaries, Miss Brown and Mrs Osbourne. They were her lifelines to the outside world.

Miss Brown took care of Mrs Dixon's correspondence, the royalties of the hymns of Dear Mr Alexander, and the Pocket Testament League, which Mrs Dixon and Dear Mr Alexander started in their young days and which was still going strong, especially in America.

I grew very fond of Miss Brown. She was one of those lovely human beings whom one meets only very seldom in a lifetime. She was goodness itself; it shone from her face.

Despite her small stature, she was like a rock to rely on and to trust, and in her quiet way she commanded respect. She was much more than the shy secretary she appeared to be at first sight.

Mrs Osbourne was much more distant and aloof. She came to the house only a couple of times a week, unlike Miss Brown who was there every weekday afternoon and stayed on nearly every evening.

Mrs Osbourne took care of the financial side of the household – the bills and accounts that Mrs Dixon knew little about. In the middle of the house, there was a secret walk-in cupboard, or safe, where all important papers and silver were kept. It was where she spent most of her time.

Mrs Osbourne arrived at the house by car, and always brought her white pink-eyed bull terrier, which was left in the vehicle.

Some say that dogs look like their owners, and in this case the eyes matched perfectly. I treated them both with great respect.

Mrs Osbourne was never one for long conversations, and although I often went to see the dog to say hello to it, I never dared to linger around the car.

Central heating in the house provided background warmth, but unfortunately it didn't reach upstairs to our floor. My room, with a north-facing window, was as "cold as a Russian hell," as we used to say in Finland.

Often the freezing and damp cold went through my bones and left me numb. It made me think of a sauna, although the dry cold in Finland never felt as cold as the dampness here. The Finnish cold made my cheeks red, not my nose. However, a warm bath was lovely on cold evenings; I'd go quickly from there to my sagging bed, which after a while enveloped me quite nicely.

Mrs Dixon had a hot water bottle, which we filled and put into her bed each evening. One day, I plucked up enough courage to ask if she had one for me, as Frieda had done much earlier. She did have one, and it was old and frail so I had to be very careful not to burst it. Still, it was better than nothing and made my life more tolerable.

Perhaps the mornings were the worst. Frieda, bless her alarm clock and punctuality, called me at 6.45am. There was no lie-in for us; in a couple of minutes, I had to be downstairs.

In my freezing cold room, I got up quickly, put on the gas fire to warm my underclothes, brushed my teeth, combed my hair and went down to the kitchen where Frieda had already put the kettle on. We made a cup of tea for ourselves and then one for the postman.

When the doorbell rang, I took the tea and some biscuits to him and greeted him, asking if there were any letters for me. His answer was always the same: "I'm very well, Miss." Except one time, he added, "I'm leaving. Retiring, you know."

"I didn't know," I said. "How nice for you. No more early mornings for you after this week. Isn't that a lovely thought?"

He replied that early mornings had never bothered him. I nearly said, "It's bothered me", and laughed all the way to the kitchen.

Once in the kitchen, I excitedly said to Frieda, "After this week, we can sleep in longer. The postman is retiring and we're not going to tell Mrs Dixon anything about it or she'll make us continue the tea ceremony for the new postman. What do you think?"

"Are you sure that's all right?" asked Frieda. "I think we should tell her," she said.

"Frieda, don't worry," I told her. "I'll take the blame for it, if it comes to that. It will be all right. You'll see. This is our chance."

We didn't tell anyone about it, because nobody asked. We felt quite daring; we'd broken an old tradition of the house. In any case, Mrs Dixon's hearing wasn't getting any better. She couldn't hear the doorbell any more, and had asked only once or twice if the postman had had his tea. Soon she forgot to ask about it altogether, and from then on we got up only to make the tea for her.

The winter added an extra year to Mrs Dixon. Her disability – her bad leg – gave her pain, which we could see etched on her face.

I'd been in Tennessee for only a couple of weeks, when suddenly one night I heard her crying for help. Without waking Frieda, I ran to Mrs Dixon's room. She was lying on her bed, crying with pain. She had cramp in her leg. I massaged it and then helped her to walk about the room. Luckily, I could understand her instructions and was able to do what she wanted.

It happened again and again, as it must have done many times before, but Frieda had never heard her crying. Mrs Dixon never mentioned these attacks in the morning. Perhaps she'd forgotten about them or thought they were a bad dream.

Mrs Dixon had an important weekly routine. Choir practice was on Monday, Tuesday and Wednesday evening, and on Thursday evenings she went to a concert at the town hall. She was very proud of her choirs: the City of Birmingham Choir, the Choral Union, and the Bach Society. Mrs Dixon would never miss a rehearsal – it was like a duty for her.

One day, I said to Frieda: "She must have a good voice if they can keep her on in the choir at her age."

"You'll hear for yourself on Tuesday afternoon, when Mrs T comes to give her a singing lesson," said Frieda. Then she added, "Anyway, the family keeps pouring money in to help the city, so nobody would dare to ask her to retire."

I was prepared for Tuesday, and hearing Mrs T's car arrive, I went to open the door for her.

"You're the new girl, aren't you?" she asked.

"Yes, I'm Kaisu," I told her.

"Kaisu," she repeated. "I've not heard that name before. How are you getting used to life here? I hope you like it."

"Yes, thank you," I answered. "I'll go and fetch Mrs Dixon for you now."

Thanking me, Mrs T picked up her music and went into the drawing room. She was a tall, slim English beauty, who obviously took her job very seriously.

I ran up the stairs, calling "Mrs Dixon! Mrs T has arrived."

"I mustn't keep her waiting," said Mrs Dixon. "Where are my sticks?"

We found her sticks, and on the way down the stairs she told me how she used to play the violin and had regular lessons.

"But look at my fingers," she said. "They're musician's fingers no more. It's the arthritis, you know," she said, sadly.

We reached the hall and Mrs Dixon went into the drawing room and closed the door securely behind her. I went back to our sitting room, but in a few minutes I went back and quietly opened the hall door.

Mrs Dixon was singing the scales, up and down, her voice breaking badly and sounding not unlike a hoarse tomcat in the spring. Though it was too funny for words, I felt sorry for Mrs T, who had to come to listen to this, week after week, for years.

"I heard it once," Frieda said, "and I can't listen to it any more."

I could understand that!

Mrs Smith came as a lady-in-waiting to help Mrs Dixon get ready, escort her to the choir practice and then back home again after 9 o'clock in the evening. Mrs Smith always arrived early but knew that they would be late, as usual.

There was always a last-minute rush but Mrs Smith took it all calmly and sensibly, as it was nothing new to her. She was a placid, strong-looking Scottish widow in her early 60s. She greeted me as if I were an old friend, and started to tell us about last week's rehearsal. Life was fun for her.

The car was standing in the front drive, and Mr Knight was waiting in the kitchen for the signal. At last they were ready, and Mr Knight hurried out to open the car doors and help Mrs Dixon in.

After taking them to town, Mr Knight was sent home as Mrs Dixon felt it was too long for him to wait. So they always came home by bus, which dropped them in the main street at the top of our road.

We girls were there to open the door to them. Mrs Smith left straight away to walk home. Mrs Dixon had her eggs to wash, and we had to wait to hear how the rehearsal had gone.

Chapter 7

On one of my first days in the house, I'd been taken with my duster to do the breakfast room, which was really more like a library, with its bound volumes of various religious periodicals and other heavy old books.

I suddenly heard the telephone ringing. "The telephone!" I thought. "Now where is it?" I'd forgotten to ask about it. I remembered the captain had phoned here, when we arrived in England, but I hadn't yet seen it.

"It's here in this cupboard – I'll answer it," called Mrs Allen, as she opened a small door under the grand staircase.

It revealed a small space with a sloping ceiling, full of old periodicals. There was just enough room for a stool, a tiny shelf, and just as tiny a window.

The telephone stood on the shelf. I'd never seen such an ancient one, except in films. It was a real museum piece. It was tall with a round brass base and a speaker on the top. There was a hook on the side from which hung the earpiece. It was ringing hoarsely.

Mrs Allen somehow managed to squeeze herself onto the stool. She took up the earpiece and shouted, "'Allo, 'allo" for a long time, and then, "Mrs Dixon? Yes certainly. Just a moment." Turning to us, she said: "Go quickly and ask Mrs Dixon to come to the phone."

I ran up the stairs like lightning, and as quickly came down again to shout my answer into this wonderful instrument.

"Mrs Dixon is coming. Can you wait a moment, please?"

By the time Mrs Dixon finally came to the phone, we were already having our elevenses and laughing about the antique object.

Mrs Meyer prepared us for our weekly trial – cooking the Sunday lunch. She had brought a tin of peas and carrots, a few extra potatoes, and more sausages just in case the delivered ones in the pantry weren't enough. There was already a tin of peaches and custard powder in the cupboard. There was nothing for me to worry about – Frieda was going to show me the art of cooking. After all, she had been taught by a real cookery teacher.

It was a triumph. Neither the mashed potatoes nor the custard had any lumps, and the sausages were fried to perfection. However, even a simple meal tastes better when it is served in a grand manner at a large dining table. I laid the white cloth, went to fetch snowdrops from the garden, and finally played the xylophone for lunch.

"We'll leave the dishes and plates on the food warmer," said Frieda. "You'll soon see why."

I helped her carry in the covered dishes.

Eventually, Mrs Dixon arrived in her usual blue dress, which had the week's menu in spots on her bosom. She was smiling.

"It's already lunchtime," she said. "How the time flies. How are my little daughters this morning?" she asked, giving us a hearty laugh.

We were standing on either side of her at the table and sat down after her. Mrs Dixon clasped her hands together on the table and bowed her head – an example that we followed – and then she started her long grace.

Perhaps she'd forgotten what she had already said at the beginning, because she repeated most of it. At last it finished and we could start to serve her first, before helping ourselves. It was a good lunch, and even the Bisto gravy, which I experienced for the first time, was very tasty.

On Sundays, we always had a proper sit-down tea in the dining room. Frieda and I laid the table again. We buttered bread to have with jam and ham, which had been waiting in the pantry for the past three days. There were also some biscuits and sometimes plain cakes.

Frieda had told me that Mrs Dixon's old secretary, Miss E, always came for Sunday tea, so when the doorbell rang, I went to the hall to open the door for her.

"Good afternoon," she said. "Here I am again. It's still cold but I suppose you're quite used to this weather."

She took off her coat, scarf and hat. She was small, neat and round, with a round face and pinkish-coloured, thin hair in small curls, except at the top where it was flat and straight.

"You must be the new girl here," she said to me. "It's so necessary for Mrs Dixon to have at least a couple of girls in the house. I trust you're taking good care of her." She finished by saying, "Don't bother to go upstairs to tell her I've arrived. I'll go and see her myself." She started to climb the grand staircase.

After a while, they came down to the dining room and we brought the tea in. Mrs Dixon again said grace and then poured the tea for us all. Miss E led the conversation by asking in her clear voice about us and our families. She was a good listener and seemed to be genuinely interested in us. She made fair comments and inspired us so much that we soon started to look forward to her Sunday visits. After tea, both she and Mrs Dixon retired to the drawing room while we went to our own room to read.

Much later in the evening, after supper, the eggs had to be washed and counted, recorded in the book, and finally taken down to the cellar. Without being asked, we used to wait until Mrs Dixon had done all that and come up again from the cellar, for fear that she might harm herself on those rickety steps.

We then went to the kitchen to say goodnight, which used to take a long time as we had to hear the story of the day's happenings or of the olden days, or the number of eggs and how dirty they were.

At last we said goodnight, hugged and kissed and received her blessing. I soon started to get used to this slow routine.

Perhaps the highlight of each day was the lunch, and a chat with Mrs Meyer. We soon found out that she and her family were staunch supporters of the Socialist Party, and we later recognised them as fashionable and intellectual socialists. It made the discussion more interesting, as I was a true blue Conservative. Otherwise, the politics of the house were very liberal, but the subject was never discussed.

Morals were important. Very bad things – and never, ever mentioned – were drinking, smoking, sex and divorce. Television was bad and corrupting, but radio was just about accepted, for our sake and for us alone.

When I got to know Mrs Dixon better, I teased her a couple of times about a large photograph she had of the Queen, hanging on the wall opposite the butler's pantry.

"Don't you think the Queen has painted lips in the photograph?" I would tease.

"How could you say such a thing about our Queen!" Mrs Dixon would exclaim indignantly. "Of course she wouldn't do anything of the kind. She wouldn't be so wicked. She is young and beautiful without any paint."

There was still one room in the house that I hadn't yet seen – Miss Brown's office. It took quite a few days before I found enough courage to ask Miss Brown if Frieda and I could both see it.

"Of course. Any time," said Miss Brown. "I'll be in there if I'm not in the nursery, or in the study with Mrs Dixon."

Miss Brown's office was at the dark end of our corridor, where the floorboards creaked loudly. We knocked on the door and heard her call to us to come in. Opening the door, I said, "I hope we're not disturbing you."

49

"Not at all," Miss Brown smiled. "I've only a few royalties to sort out."

She was sitting at an ancient typewriter by a small window in the dark, dank office. It was only dimly lit, and as my eyes slowly became used to the gloom I saw, to my horror, the dustiest and dirtiest office I could ever have imagined.

The window had no curtains and was small and so dirty that hardly any light came through it. The only artificial light came from a bare bulb hanging over a large table in the middle of the room. This table was piled high with books and papers, all black and yellow with dust and age.

All around the room were very roughly-made shelves, each filled with yet more papers. On the floor was a threadbare carpet, not large enough to cover the dirty floorboards, and from which the remaining pattern had long ago disappeared under layers of dust.

On this carpet stood a rusty enamelled bowl.

"That's there because the roof leaks," said Miss Brown, almost casually, when I asked her about it. Sure enough, there was a large hole in the ceiling and the lining paper – discoloured by water leaks and dirt – was hanging down into the room.

Miss Brown saw us standing there, looking about us, speechless with horror.

"Isn't it a bit cold for you to work in here?" I finally asked, having seen a rusty old electric heater with only one bar working.

"I'm quite used to it," she replied. "Sometimes I go into the nursery to warm up."

I asked about the large quantity of papers.

"They're letters about Mr Alexander's hymns," said Miss Brown. "We get the royalties when they're copied, although sometimes we run into difficulties about getting the money."

50

Poor Miss Brown. She never complained about her work or the state of her office. Mrs Dixon never went into it and nobody every cleaned it.

Cold shivers went through me; sad shivers of disgust about the state of the room, despite all the money in the downstairs safety cupboard. I was surprised that Miss Brown actually survived and was healthy. Perhaps she tried to disturb the dust as little as possible, and left the papers and books alone. Even Scrooge's counting house couldn't have been more melancholy than this inner sanctum of Mr Alexander's hymns.

Once, I said to her, "Poor Miss Brown. You really should have a better office."

Her only reply was, "It's quite all right. I wouldn't worry Mrs Dixon with it."

Slowly, we got to know the house better. There were so many old, mysterious things to discover – we listened to Mrs Dixon endlessly telling us about their histories. She was very fond of her sentimental memories, of her missionary friends, her family, and – of course – Dear Mr Alexander.

She still had three members of her family; two sisters, and a half brother who, with his white beard, looked like a handsome Father Christmas. He came a few times to visit Mrs Dixon, but never stayed more than half an hour.

Frieda was already attending English classes in town once a week, and now I was glad to join her.

"I don't like Frieda going to town alone," Mrs Dixon said to us one day. "It's much better that you go together and look after each other. But remember – you must be back by 10 o'clock and don't talk to any strangers. I know the world is full of bad men."

Her voice had dropped almost to a whisper as she said this, as if it were a sin even to mention such things. She had forgotten that Frieda and I had each travelled a long way to be here, without getting ourselves into any tricky situations.

We just nodded in agreement, assured her that we would look after each other, and went to catch the bus into town.

Frieda had made a few friends there, and after class I went with her to meet them and have a cup of coffee. Much later, two Finnish girls joined the class, and we eagerly exchanged news from home and compared our experiences here in England.

The lessons must have helped, because soon I could even start to understand our next-door neighbour, Mr X, who lived with his mother in the large house next door and kept his car in our garages. He was a very handsome, well-dressed and obviously cultured man in his late 30s, but he was intensely shy and had a bad stutter.

I liked him, and tried to be in the kitchen in the evenings when he returned the garage keys. I would ask him the name of the beautiful tree at the end of the garden, or enquire whether he'd had a busy day.

His answers were slow but his smile was appealing. When I realised he was embarrassed by my innocent intentions, I stopped going to see him in the kitchen, although I'm sure I'd helped his confidence by talking to him.

Chapter 8

The garden was my delight, and I often walked there in the afternoons, enjoying its beauty and solitude.

The thrushes and robins were already starting to claim their own territories, singing their hearts out. The winter flowering cherries were nearly over, and the daffodils were getting taller under the trees. Villis, the gardener, was busy planting and trimming the bushes. The sunken garden had been tidied and was partly in bloom, while the rest of the garden was awakening and bursting into life.

I loved this slow expectation of summer. It was so different from Finland, where the snow stayed long into spring and suddenly melted; then, in the space of just a couple of weeks, the world was green and summer had arrived.

I told Mrs Dixon how much I enjoyed the sunny spring days in her English garden and how much time I spent there instead of reading English.

"Well, when it's bluebell time, you and Frieda must go to the Lickey Hills," she said. "The whole forest is blue with flowers. That area used to belong to our family but I think they've now given it to the city so everyone can enjoy its beauty."

She reminded me that the bluebells weren't to be picked.

"I remember that, when I was a little girl, we used to go there for picnics," she added. "It was far out of town then, of course. What lovely times we used to have, and how nice that it's now preserved and used."

Mrs Dixon's choir was practising Michael Tippett's work "Child of Our Time" for the spring concert in the town hall.

The day before the concert, I saw Miss Brown and Mrs Dixon looking for a white dress that hung in the mahogany wardrobe on the landing. There were two white dresses, each equally old and shabby. Some 30 years earlier, they must have been beautiful.

On the night of the performance. Mrs Smith arrived early. Mr Knight was there, too, in his dark suit with his PTL cap, waiting for the ladies.

Panic started after Mrs Dixon spent too long having tea – they were going to be late again.

In the study, Mrs Smith and Miss Brown were trying to organise Mrs Dixon and dress her. I was there too, supposedly to help, but really I didn't want to miss the fun.

At last they managed to pull the dress over Mrs Dixon's head, but the garment was too tight and too long. It had a long train that I had to pin up and tack into place to avoid Mrs Dixon tangling her bad leg in it.

We were all hot and bothered, and Mrs Dixon had to go and wash her face for a second time, to cool down. Then her hair had to be done again. Unfortunately, there was no perfume to drown the scent of sweat and old mothballs.

We had to find her a clean hanky, her handbag, and dust her shoes. Then we realised one of her walking sticks was missing – I found it in the nursery. After that, she had to be helped into her coat and hat.

At long last, they were ready to go. Outside, we had difficulty getting her into the car because of her tight dress, but at last even that was successfully managed. For safety, Mrs Smith was carrying the music.

This time, Mr Knight waited for them throughout the concert and brought them safely back again, stopping on the way to take Mrs Smith home as she wasn't allowed to walk alone in the streets so late in the evening.

It was nearly 11 o'clock when I went to help Mrs Dixon unpin and undress. But she then put on another dress as she had work to do – cleaning the eggs!

While she did that job, she told me about how enjoyable and magnificent a concert it had been. Although she didn't care much for modern music, she said, it had been an interesting work to sing.

When Mrs Smith came next time, we heard the real story. We'd guessed right – they'd arrived late. The choir was already on the platform in the town hall and everyone was waiting for her. The conductor, deciding he could wait no longer, had taken his bow and received his applause – he was just about to start when he saw Mrs Dixon arrive, walking with her sticks and holding large sheets of music.

She had given the conductor a faint smile, and continued her noisy journey towards the choir platform. Once there, she tried to get up the steps but was prevented by her tight dress and her disability. Several singers came down to help her – some holding her arms, some pushing from the back, some lifting the hem of her dress, and some holding her sticks and music.

Once in place, she then had to stand for far too long on her bad leg. It must have been a tiresome and painful evening for her. No wonder her singing was now worse than ever – the choir apparently tried to cover her by singing even louder. But Mrs Dixon suffered gladly for the sake of art and the joy of singing. Soon afterwards, I heard that a vote had been cast in favour of her retirement but no-one dared tell her.

One Sunday teatime a few weeks after my arrival, Mrs Dixon's old secretary Miss E had a bright idea.

"Frieda and Kaisu should go to church on Sunday mornings. It would be so good for their English language," she said.

Frieda and I agreed that we would try it to see how we got on. Mrs Dixon, who seemed anxious that we should speak English fluently, lent the scheme her support. She had her favourite church in mind for us, although we couldn't attend Holy Communion, but we had a better idea.

"Why shouldn't we try a different church each Sunday?" I suggested. "We wouldn't get bored and we'd be able to compare the different architecture."

So the following Sunday, after breakfast, we went to our nearest church, which happened to be the Scottish Presbyterian Church. It wasn't very old but it was built in traditional style.

It was a lovely sunny morning. The trees were showing buds of delicate green, the crocuses and daffodils were fully opened in the gardens, and the birds were singing their hearts out, calling to their mates. God's earth seemed all peace and happiness.

I was quite excited about going to church, walking there with Frieda, both of us in our Sunday best.

"Let's go as near to the front as possible. Perhaps we'll be able to understand better if we can see it well," said Frieda as she took my hand. But the church was already very full and the only seats we could find were in the middle. Soon, all the pews were full.

We sang the hymns and then settled down to listen to the long sermon, delivered from the pulpit by a strict-looking minister. Although we were listening intently, a couple of times I had to turn to Frieda – who understood the Scottish accent better than I did – and ask what the minister had said.

"Later – I'll tell you later," she said.

The sermon about sins and forgiveness went on and on. At last it was over but the minister didn't leave the pulpit. He just stood there for what seemed like ages, looking straight at us with his piercing eyes. Suddenly, he lifted his hand and pointed a finger at us, declaring loudly, "In this church, only one person speaks at a time."

There was a deathly silence, during which the congregation turned to stare at us. Now I realised that his words were directed at us, and I turned to Frieda.

"What did he say?" I asked her.

Without answering, Frieda jumped up, took my hand, and said loudly, "Come! Come!"

By then, everyone was staring at us as we struggled out of the pew. Frieda was still holding my hand as we fled towards the door, but then we heard footsteps behind us. Suddenly, Frieda stopped and turned around, facing the people who had followed us. She shouted at them, "She hasn't been in England very long and couldn't understand what the minister was saying!"

With that, she turned again, still holding my hand, and we walked out. The people called to us that they understood and would tell the minister. Hearing this, Frieda turned towards them again, gave a long look at the minister still standing in his pulpit, and shouted, "Don't bother!"

Looking horrified, people called after us, "Please come again!" But Frieda told me not to look back, and we went out through the gates, onto the street, and home again.

Once out of sight of the church, I burst out laughing.

"Frieda, you were priceless. It was so funny!" But Frieda was upset.

I eventually managed to get her to see the funny side of it, and Mrs Dixon laughed heartily about it many times. But the experience ended our churchgoing – Frieda wasn't going to risk another upset like that.

A cold spell followed those few lovely days. Frieda caught a cold and took to her bed for a day or two. Though she claimed not to like the idea, the temptation of lying snugly in a warm bed was too much for her to resist.

"I can't be of much help in any case," she said.

I went to see that she had enough blankets, filled her hot water bottle, and gave her aspirin. She was soon up and about again. Then she started to complain of stomach pains. Poor Frieda looked really ill and was obviously suffering. She went back to bed again, and when I went in to see her she was crying quietly and refused all offers of food.

I went to tell Mrs Dixon, and Miss Brown phoned Dr Preston, Mrs Dixon's doctor, who kept a few private patients on his list despite the fact he was retired.

Within half an hour, he was at the door. Although Dotty was in the house that day, I happened to open the door to him. He looked every inch the part – a small, trim man in a dark suit and a stiff white collar that seemed to keep his chin up. His face was large and quite ugly, but not unpleasant.

"My name is Dr Preston," he announced. "I believe that you have a patient here for me."

Dotty had come to stand behind me, and answered his greeting.

"Yes sir. Madam is worried about one of the girls. Would you please come upstairs and see Madam about it?"

"Certainly," replied Dr Preston, as he handed Dotty his Gladstone bag and started to walk up the stairs.

Dotty was following him in her long blue dress and long white apron, and despite her 80 years she was carrying the doctor's bag as she had so many times before.

I stood at the bottom of the stairs watching them. They seemed to belong to a different era. The time difference had vanished and I was looking at life as it used to be in this house.

After a long discussion in Mrs Dixon's study, Dotty took Dr Preston to the top floor to see Frieda. After examining her, he decided to send her to hospital for tests, just in case.

Next morning, Mr Knight was waiting with Mrs Osbourne, Mrs Dixon's financial secretary, for Frieda to get ready to go to hospital. Frieda felt much better by now and was even smiling at the thought of a drive in the old Ford.

"I hope it won't shake your insides too much," I said, walking with her to the car.

Dr Preston had arranged for Frieda to be examined straight away, and in a couple of hours she was back home in bed. The test results came later – she had a grumbling appendix.

Frieda felt much better after this news, and was up the next day helping us to dust, although she still felt weak. She was sitting with us after lunch, when Mrs Dixon came in to see how she was.

"I'm better," she told Mrs Dixon, before suddenly bursting into tears.

"What is it, my child?" asked Mrs Dixon, almost as surprised as I was. "I don't think you should be up yet," she told her.

"No, I should be in bed," sobbed Frieda. "I have done a special favour by getting up early and helping you, and I've had no thanks for it. I've done my job well but you've said nothing – you've not even noticed. I want to be thanked because I've done more than I should."

After this outburst, Frieda was crying hysterically, with tears running down her reddened cheeks.

"But of course I recognise your work and I'm very grateful that thou art here, staying with me. I couldn't manage without thee, my darling Frieda," Mrs Dixon said, trying to calm the sobbing girl.

"I'm not darling Frieda – I'm only someone who does work for you and doesn't get thanks for it," Frieda cried.

I felt sorry for both of them. I looked at Mrs Dixon and said, "I think you're right. Frieda should still be in bed."

I took Frieda by the arm and said to her, "Come. You aren't well. You must go back to bed for at least another day."

Frieda's outburst left all of us feeling sad. Everyone was overwhelmingly kind to her for a long time, and we were remembered more often by Mrs Dixon, who took pains to praise us. This sometimes sounded artificial to me, but Frieda thrived on it.

Chapter 9

Mrs Meyer brought her son Lukas to lunch one day. He was a gingery-blond curly-haired youth who was extremely shy and blushed every time we said something to him.

We had plenty to ask him. Did he like his English university? What did he study apart from biology? What sports did he play? What hobbies did he have?

Our questions gave Mrs Meyer a bright idea – she invited us to tea the next day, going first to ask permission from Mrs Dixon.

"How nice of you, Mrs Meyer, to think of inviting my girls to tea. Of course they can go. I'm sure they'll like it very much," said Mrs Dixon.

Next day, before we left, we prepared the tea tray for Mrs Dixon. We even put the tea in the pot, so it needed only the hot water that Miss Brown would boil later.

We girls and Mrs Meyer took a bus to the part of town where she lived – a suburb of endless streets of identical semi-detached houses. From the outside, her house looked like all the others in the long street, but on the inside it had an air of culture. The longest walls were filled with bookshelves – the Meyers were obviously a very literary family.

It was an interesting afternoon. We heard many new stories about English life, and about their suburb. They felt as much apart from it as they were from their own country of Austria. One thing I never really discovered was why they had come to live in England in the first place, especially as Mr Meyer didn't even teach German.

By the next day, I knew I'd caught Frieda's cold. It seemed to get worse towards the evening, by which time I had a sore throat, aching chest and head, and I felt very hot. I went to bed early that evening, and by the morning, I felt worse. I couldn't face food but Frieda's cup of tea made my chest feel better.

This time, Mrs Dixon didn't want to delay calling in Dr Preston. Soon, she and Miss Brown brought him to my cold, dark bedroom. Miss Brown kept her distance while Mrs Dixon hovered around me. Dr Preston examined my throat and took my temperature.

"There's nothing much wrong with you – just a little bronchitis and influenza. You'll be all right very soon," he said.

I looked at him through sore, watery eyes and felt terribly ill. I shouted at him, "But I feel so ill! I am ill!"

Immediately, I felt ashamed of my outburst. I wanted to hide from their stares. So I pulled the sheet up over my face. There was a dreadful tearing noise, and to my utter surprise I was looking at my visitors through a big hole I'd just torn in the sheet. The hole was immediately in front of my face, and my horrified eyes scanned the room, ending at Mrs Dixon.

"Oh dear!" I exclaimed. "I'm sorry. So very sorry."

Suddenly, everyone burst out laughing, while I was still trying to apologise.

"I'll mend it when I'm better," I said.

Trying to hide her smile, Mrs Dixon said that Frieda would bring me another sheet and plenty of hot drinks to make me feel better. Miss Brown was still giggling as she left the room.

I got better soon, and to speed my recovery Mrs Meyer came with a message that Lukas would like to take me to the pictures to see a film that Frieda had already seen. Mrs Meyer said she should go and ask Mrs Dixon's permission.

"Oh no! Please don't ask her," I said, starting to panic. "She'll never agree. I'll think of another way to arrange it, because I really want to see the film."

Frieda, true to her kind personality, was not at all jealous that I was going out with Lukas. On the contrary, she helped me think of a way to get out of the house secretly.

"I'll pretend I have a headache and want to go to bed early," I suggested. Frieda agreed.

"I'll walk up the stairs so she thinks it's you going up to bed," she said.

"And the meantime, I'll go into the laundry room to change," I told her. "Mrs Dixon never goes in there so I should be safe."

Suddenly, I worried about being able to get back into the house again. Frieda was more than helpful.

"I'll stay awake," she said, "and when you get back, just throw a stone up at my window and I'll come down and open the kitchen door for you."

"Sweet Frieda, you are super – I knew you'd help me," I told her, gratefully, as I hugged her.

"It's nearly as exciting for me as it is for you," she said.

The arrangements sounded foolproof. Mrs Dixon never came to our rooms, and lately we'd gone to bed early with real headaches.

"Splendid," said Mrs Meyer, when she heard our plans. "But if you're caught, don't say that I knew anything about it."

I told her I didn't want Lukas to know about my plans to get out, and asked that he should wait for me just outside, in the street.

At 8 o'clock that night, I went to the nursery looking very sorry for myself.

"I came to say goodnight because I have a dreadful headache," I told Mrs Dixon. "I'm going to have a hot bath and go to bed early."

I moved towards her to give her a kiss on the cheek, but she took my head in her hands and looked at me for a long time. In my guilty mind, it seemed an eternity.

"Poor child," she said at last. "Are you really ill? You don't feel very hot."

On hearing this, I almost blushed, my heart thumped twice as fast, and now I really did feel ill. So I could tell her, truthfully, that I really wasn't feeling well.

"Perhaps thou should have an early night, then. I hope thou will feel better tomorrow," she told me, finally.

"I'm sure I will," I answered.

"Good night. Sleep well."

I closed the nursery door and silently dashed down the stairs, while Frieda, who had been waiting outside the nursery door, walked upstairs, stepping heavily across the landing, and then turned on the bath taps in case Mrs Dixon was listening.

My clothes were already in the laundry room, and I changed into them quickly. Once outside, I crept along the wall so Mrs Dixon wouldn't see me from her window. Then I dashed to the street where Lukas was waiting for me. I took his hand and we ran to the bus stop.

At our destination, we ran into the cinema as I didn't want to risk missing any of the film. I don't think that I'd ever enjoyed a film more, with Lukas holding my hand.

We had a quick cup of coffee afterwards, while I kept my eye on the clock. Now I could tell Lukas about my secret escape.

"I guessed you'd have to come up with some tricks to get out," he said calmly, before taking me back home.

Thank goodness the kitchen was in darkness, and so was the nursery, which meant that Mrs Dixon was in her study so wouldn't be able to hear Frieda. Lukas did well to hit Frieda's window with the second stone – Frieda's face appeared as she looked out, then disappeared again.

Outside, we waited, holding our breath. Suddenly, Lukas hugged and kissed me. I could see that he was blushing more than I was.

"You will come again, won't you, please?" he asked quietly.

"Thank you, Lukas. I'd love to," I told him, before dashing back to the house.

But I never did go out with him again. It wouldn't have been the same as that first time. And I doubted if there would be any more films good enough to risk another secret escape. Anyway, Lukas's holiday soon finished and he went back to university.

One day, Mrs Dixon told us that somebody had telephoned her to say that there was a Finnish girl without a job, and asking Mrs Dixon to take her for a week or two before she returned to Finland. Mrs Dixon had said that of course she would help. There were plenty of rooms upstairs, and a little more help in the house was always welcome.

So Agnete arrived, and was put in my care. She was fat and blonde, and a strangely quiet girl who missed her home dreadfully. She worked with us but spent all her spare time in her room, where she cried a lot, making her pale eyes red, day after day. I tried to cheer her up but without much success.

She had been with an English family for three months, and in just that short space of time had put on a lot of weight. This happened to a lot of girls, who missed their own families and ate to comfort themselves.

Agnete's home was in northern Finland, where she belonged to a very strict and puritan sect. She was terribly lonely in this big town of Birmingham, where she feared she was losing her soul. A sense of sin weighed heavily on her shoulders. She had given up caring about her appearance, and all the hours spent in her room were devoted to enhancing her spiritual well-being by reading the Bible. To her, that was much more important than improving the way she looked.

One evening, she came down to the sitting room. I was there alone as Frieda had gone to have a bath. Agnete's eyes had a distant stare and they were red from crying. Her long, straight hair was hanging over her shoulders and was wet with sweaty agony and tears. She looked hot and desperate.

"I have been praying every day, praying so long, and I still feel I haven't been answered," she said with a little sob. "There is no God here. I am lost and long to be at home. I have not been blessed and my sins are overpowering me." She paused for a moment, and said to me: "Please, you must bless me. You must." She cried and sobbed helplessly.

Amazed, I said: "But I can't do that. How can I? I don't know how and I don't belong to your church sect." I tried telling her that she hadn't sinned – that it was all in her imagination. Soon she would be home and all would be well, I told her.

"But I need your blessing tonight – now – otherwise I shall die. Please bless me, please!"

She was desperate, and her despair frightened me.

"All right, I'll do it," I said. "But you must tell me how, and what to say."

She knelt in front of me, took my hand and placed it on her head, and told me to say "I bless you" loudly and many times. I did so, caressing her with my other hand. It seemed to calm her, and her sobbing was becoming quieter.

Then, limp and heavy, she buried her head in my lap. Silently I stroked her wet hair, feeling nearly as emotionally drained as she was.

At last, she whispered: "Thank you. I feel so much better and I can now sleep in peace. My sins are forgiven."

"You haven't sinned," I tried to tell her again. "You are only lonely, but soon you will be with your own people and happy again."

Finally, she went upstairs, leaving me feeling shaken at having seen the strength of another person's trust in God and salvation, and how imaginary sins could almost destroy a person. To her, the sins were real. To us, they were only wicked thoughts.

Next day, she was much brighter. She never mentioned the episode to me or to anyone else in the house. Two days later, she left us to return to Finland.

Several years later, I read in a newspaper that a fanatical puritan sect in Finland – Agnete's sect – went to their neighbours' houses and smashed all the television sets because they considered TV to be a great evil. Then they paid for the damage. Apparently, any price was worth the satisfaction it gave the sect to have tried to save their village from such an evil pastime. At least they made their point.

Perhaps I was still in a delicate frame of mind when, a couple of days later, I was quietly cleaning our sitting room, when Tigger, Mrs Dixon's 16-year-old fat cat, suddenly jumped in through the open window and presented me with a live mouse. I jumped up on the table in a flash, shouting at Tigger to take the mouse away. Tigger seemed to know exactly what I'd said, and looked at me with disappointed eyes because I didn't appreciate his present. He showed off and played with the poor mouse, which must have been even more frightened than I was.

Frieda heard me shouting, and came in to see what was happening. She left the door open, and Tigger saw his chance. He picked up the mouse and ran to the nursery to see if his mistress would like his present better than I did.

Mrs Dixon saw Tigger coming in but hadn't noticed the mouse, which soon saw an escape route through the furniture and quickly vanished somewhere in the building.

After that, Tigger brought in birds and mice several times, but by then I'd got used to his offerings and saved them from his old claws when I could.

We told Mrs Dixon about the mouse in the house. She wasn't at all worried – in fact, she laughed about it.

"Tigger is such a funny cat," she said. "He's so proud of his catches and loves to show off the fact that he can still hunt, in spite of his age and weight."

Looking lovingly at her old companion, she said, in a mock scold, "Oh Tigger, Tigger, you naughty, naughty cat." Tigger just purred as he accepted the compliment.

Villis, the gardener, also had a cat – a timid female that produced a litter of kittens in the spring. They were soft, delicate little balls of fur and it was impossible not to love them. I took some of them onto the lawn, in the sunshine, and they followed me as I was the only moving object. They didn't like to be alone in the big world.

After I returned them to their mother, I continued my walk in the garden. How I enjoyed the delicate green of the new leaves, the yellow of the daffodils, and the various reds of the proud tulips.

I walked round the duck pond to the summerhouse. There, I saw an elderly, sophisticated lady sitting in a deck chair. I'd never seen her before. We greeted each other, but she obviously wanted to strike up a conversation with me.

"You don't know who I am but I know that you're one of the girls from the house. Where do you come from?" she asked me, in a strong French accent.

"Finland," I replied.

"Oh Finland!" she said, in surprise. "That's so far away and so cold. I am also a foreigner. I come from France but I've lived here for many years. I married an Englishman. He's dead now and I am alone. Mrs Dixon has given me permission to come here at any time and enjoy this wonderful garden. I bring my deckchair and my book and I am in heaven."

I told her that we had such luxuries as deckchairs in the house, and we both laughed.

I met her there a few times afterwards, and she told me her life story, in her strong, delightful French accent. She was a pianist but had given up public performances after she married.

I told her how poor my French was but I still remembered a few French songs and we sang "Parlez mois d'amour" together.

"Magnifique!" she cried, remembering her own youth.

Then, just as quietly as she'd come, she walked out of the garden, waving her hand in au revoir.

Chapter 10

There wasn't much chance of escaping the house for long, but when an opportunity arose, I bravely took it. Of course, I had to tell a lie to escape, but it was worth it.

Perhaps the worst of it was that I didn't tell the truth to anyone in the house – which was that my Finnish ex-boyfriend was coming to London and wanted to meet me there at the weekend. Telling my lie, I changed him into a female cousin. This so-called cousin had written to confirm where he was staying – I would be staying at the same hotel, too.

Mrs Dixon wasn't particularly concerned about the name of the hotel. She was far more interested in the Finnish periodical that I'd received with the letter, and she lingered on the page that had portrait photographs of people who had recently celebrated "round" birthdays. She just wanted to see what older Finnish people looked like, as she'd seen only younger ones. After a long discussion about Finns, she gave me permission to go.

I was naturally very excited to be taking a train to London, although it was an icy cold Saturday afternoon. Everything had been arranged, and my ex-boyfriend was at the station to meet me. How funny it was to be speaking Finnish again, and to hear even the smallest item of news – so important when one is far away from friends.

London was no longer a strange place to me, and I loved to see it again and do as much sight-seeing as possible. In the evening, we met some of his friends and dined together in the West End. Although we'd grown distant from each other, it was nice to refresh memories and enjoy the company and excitement of meeting different people.

Sunday morning was spent visiting Westminster Abbey and seeing the changing of the guard at Buckingham Palace. Then, after a good lunch, he left for Helsinki.

I was alone in London and had three hours to spare before my train took me back to Birmingham. In a Sunday paper, I'd seen an advert seeking an au pair girl in Hendon. I decided to try my luck, to see if I could move to London. Life in the capital seemed to be so much more exciting than in our "prison".

I soon found that the quickest way to Hendon was by underground train. Hendon looked like a prosperous suburb and the house wasn't far from the station.

The door was opened by a smart and pleasant-looking woman, who was clearly the lady of the house. I showed her the newspaper, told her I was looking for a job, and apologised for coming on a Sunday.

"That's perfectly all right," she said. "The sooner the better. Do come in and we'll have a little talk. Do you already have a place?" she asked.

"Yes, I do, but not in London and it's with an old lady," I told her.

Asking me to sit down, she continued, "We have a German girl here, helping us with two children. She does all the washing and cleaning, helps with the cooking, and looks after the young children. She doesn't have much time left for herself."

Pausing to light a cigarette, she went on, "She's been a wonderful worker and now I'm looking for someone as good as her."

She took a long look at me. I suddenly felt awkward about asking for work in such a busy household, and I looked away from her to study the room.

At last, I managed to say, "Perhaps I could manage all those duties, and I do like children."

She answered quickly: "I don't think that is enough. We need a strong girl here and I can see from your hands that you're not used to working. It wouldn't be right for you to even try to manage here. Sorry, but you're not a suitable person for us."

I was sure she was right, and I felt enormously relieved. As I got up, I saw her looking at my fur coat.

"I'm sorry – I hope you will find someone good and strong," I said.

As I left, I looked back at the pleasant house and imagined all the work within it. Then I said goodbye to the thought of living in London. Frieda was right. There was no place like "Tennessee" and we were the lucky ones.

Now I was going back to that large, quiet house, where life had stopped decades ago and nothing ever happened. From now on, I vowed that I wouldn't complain about my existence and that London would remain only on my visiting list.

I was back home before supper and I didn't tell anyone about had happened.

"Frieda, you were so right. 'Tennessee' is a good place for us," I told her that evening. "One can appreciate it even more after a visit to London. I must go and tell Mrs Dixon."

Truthfully, I was very glad to be back, and I was happy to tell Mrs Dixon about all the sightseeing I'd done.

"I think we should get to know London," I suggested. "Historically, it's a most interesting place," I added, trying to convince her.

After the freezing cold weather of my London weekend, the temperature turned warmer again. One day, Mrs Meyer brought some maps of the Midlands to show us, and when she told us about the history and beauty of the towns, we became very interested.

"We must go and see some of these places, Frieda," I exclaimed.

Frieda was equally enthusiastic. "I'm always willing to go and explore. We can do it tomorrow if you like," she said.

Mrs Meyer offered to make sure that Mrs Dixon had her lunch.

"You'll need a whole day for your trip," she said. "And we need to plan your route."

Once we'd decided where to go, we all rushed upstairs to ask Mrs Dixon if we could have the day off to go to Worcester and the Cotswolds. Frieda and I left Mrs Meyer to fill in the details for us and do the lengthy planning and organising of life in the house during our absence.

"Just think. Evesham, Broadway, Chipping Campden and Stratford," mused Frieda while she dried the lunch dishes. "That's a lot to see in one day. We must start as early as possible, and get our sandwiches prepared the night before."

I was just draining the water from the sink when Mrs Meyer came back down to the kitchen.

"It's all organised for the day after tomorrow," she announced. "It's best to go now while the weather is so lovely. I must go home now – I'll see you tomorrow, girls."

We were determined to catch the first bus of the day to Worcester. Mrs Allen had come early to make our breakfast – she had insisted on it, and even promised to do all the dusting for us that day. Wearing comfortable walking shoes and carrying our bacon sandwiches, we waved her goodbye.

We caught the bus to Worcester and walked around the town. We were charmed by the little black-and-white houses near the cathedral. The contrast between the buildings was so striking – next to the houses, God's temple was immense and seemed to reach to heaven. With King John's tomb inside, the cathedral impressed me so much I still think of it as one of the most beautiful in the country.

Not far from it was the china factory, where we saw porcelain being painted by hand. This was of especial interest to me as this type of delicate painting used to be my hobby when I lived in Helsinki.

My aunt had done it since she was young, and nearly all the porcelain in her home had been beautifully painted by her.

After a cup of coffee, we were off again, this time to Evesham. Our route took us through the sunny green countryside, and then we travelled on to Broadway, which we thought was delightful.

It was difficult to get a bus from Broadway to Chipping Campden, so we decided to walk. After buying two small bottles of lemonade, we started to climb the hill out of Broadway.

Soon, we were carrying our coats, too, as the day become hotter. The countryside looked at its best, with the wheat already tall enough to wave in the gentle breeze. Spring flowers were in their splendour along the roadsides, and the birds were busy building their nests. All this beauty was ours.

The only other person we saw was an old man, cutting the hedge beside the road. As we approached, he stopped working, wiped his brow with his arm, and said, "Ah! A lovely day again. Where are you young ladies going?"

"We're going to Chipping Campden," we replied.

"So you're walking there," he said. "It's hot work, and you've got quite a bit to go yet."

We told him we weren't at all tired.

"Are the young ladies American, or what?" he asked with a smile.

"No, I'm German and she's a Finn," Frieda told him.

"Oh. A German," he said, surprised. "Oh well. Mind how you go."

After that, we had the road to ourselves. We stopped for our packed lunch, sitting on our coats that we spread on the fresh-smelling spring grass. Afterwards, we lay on our backs looking at a lone cloud that was slowly changing its shape in the perfect blue sky. The world was sweet for us.

We reached Chipping Campden in good time, and had a pot of tea and cakes in a homely tea-room. We thought this town was even prettier than Broadway, and the old Cotswold stone houses looked comforting and cosy.

Then we took a bus to Stratford-upon-Avon, and spent an hour trying to see as much as we could of this town of Shakespeare's.

On the bus on the way home, we promised ourselves that we would return. It was already getting dark, but still well before 10 o'clock when we reached home, tired but happy.

We had so much to tell Mrs Dixon while she was cleaning her eggs.

"I'm going to write to my friends in Finland about the fruit trees in the Vale of Evesham, the glorious cathedral in Worcester, the Beacon Tower above Broadway, and the magnificent view. And of course, there's Stratford," I told her, eagerly. It all gave us the inspiration to plan further trips.

"I would love to go to Scotland," Frieda said one day. "I think we're due for a holiday soon. We could easily spend it there and see the Lake District on the way. Klaudia is coming soon to join us in the house, so she could take care of Mrs Dixon while we are away."

"What a lovely idea," I said. "But do we have enough money? I'm already thinking of the hotel bills."

Mrs Meyer suggested that we stay in youth hostels, and hitchhike for part of the journey. She convinced me that it would be safe.

"I'll lend you rucksacks. We're ramblers in our family so we have several," she said.

We allowed ourselves to think about the trip, started to read about the places we'd see, and study the maps.

Chapter 11

In spite of all this talk and planning, there was something much more important about to happen: the coronation of the Queen of England.

The newspapers were full of speculation about what the Queen was going to wear, and we eagerly studied the history of the ceremonial proceedings.

Mrs Dixon saw our enthusiasm and, as an enormous concession, decided to rent a television for the day so we could see the ceremony live. Then she came to our sitting room to tell us that she'd asked a friend of the family – a local vicar – to take Frieda and me to London the day after the coronation.

From the morning of the coronation until last thing in the evening, we sat in front of the precious television in our sitting room.

The vegetables were hastily prepared, Mrs Dixon's lunch was served at running speed, and all the dishes were left unwashed until the television schedule allowed us time to do them. Mrs Dixon didn't even come to see the evil television but we were enraptured by everything it showed us.

The coronation was much more grand and emotional – and beautifully rehearsed – than I'd ever imagined. We felt sorry for the people standing in the wet weather, but it didn't seem to dampen their enthusiasm. England was going to have another glorious Elizabethan era.

Next morning, we were up early and dressed for London – and rain. We had a quick breakfast and took the bus to the station. There we met the vicar and his daughter, who were waiting for us.

"Hello both," the vicar greeted us. "So you're the young ladies Mrs Dixon has entrusted to our care?"

Before we could answer, he continued, "This is Brenda, my daughter, and I know that you are Frieda and Kaisu. I believe that Kaisu is the same as Catherine, so if I forget the name Kaisu, I shall call you Kate. Is that all right? You can call me Father. And now we're going to see London in all its glory."

"It is very kind of Mrs Dixon to let us go, and for you to take us to London," I replied at last.

"Yes, thank you so much," added Frieda.

"That's all right – we'll enjoy it just as much, won't we, Brenda?" he said, hugging his daughter.

Brenda was mentally a little slow. She didn't take much part in the conversation but she listened intently. The train journey went quickly as the vicar told us his impressions of the coronation and explained what we were about to see in London. He seemed to be just as excited about it as we were.

The weather in London was still cold but it had stopped raining. We walked to our hotel near Russell Square, and left our cases there. The hotel was run by the Salvation Army and long before had been a row of terraced Georgian houses. Our rooms were on the top floor, at the end of a long, narrow, uneven corridor.

"I feel seasick walking along this uneven floor," I laughed to Frieda.

My room was next to Frieda's. It was small and plain, but adequate. I had just put my case down when I heard a crash and a cry from Frieda's room.

"Kaisu! Come quickly! Help me!" she cried.

I ran into her room but couldn't see Frieda, although I could hear her voice. She was on the floor with the wardrobe on top of her – the door was open and poor Frieda was trapped inside.

"What on earth are you doing in there?" I asked.

"Just get me out and I'll tell you," came the voice.

I could hardly push the wardrobe up for laughing. I tried to be serious.

"I hope you're all right. If not, you won't be able to see the Queen," I said.

She checked to make sure she wasn't hurt, and explained that she'd hung her coat on the open door of the wardrobe, knelt with her back to it to do up her shoelaces, and it had fallen over on top of her.

"The coat was too heavy for it, and on this uneven floor it just fell over," she said.

"Thank goodness you're not hurt," I said. "Now we must hurry to get an early lunch before joining the crowds."

Father had obviously been in our chosen restaurant before. He ordered lunch, which we enjoyed very much, and then we took a bus to Parliament Square.

The West End was full of people. I'd never seen such vast crowds in my entire life. People were singing and shouting, and some were wearing fancy hats, waving flags and carrying balloons.

We pushed our way through them and somehow got into Westminster Abbey. Everything was just as it had been when we'd seen it on television the day before – the decorations, the flowers, the carpet, and even the organ playing. There were very few other people in the abbey.

Walking down the aisle, I tried to imagine how the Queen must have felt the day before. That young woman, wearing the Imperial State Crown, had walked along the very same carpet. Her promise of a lifetime's service to her people, and her sense of duty and devotion, must have filled her mind.

Our own minds were filled with the seriousness and grace of that great occasion and the sense of history. Time had changed Britain – perhaps more than many countries – but the Queen has not changed. She is still scrupulously fulfilling her promise and doing her duty.

Standing near the altar and hearing the great organ playing, I could see the coronation all over again, as I'd watched it on television the day before. I looked at the coronation chair, where the Queen had humbly bowed her head. Now I crossed my fingers and also humbly begged that she be granted a long and happy life.

From the Abbey, we went to the cloisters – or, as it looked to me, back stage. There was a small hut with a notice on the door that said "Peers Only". I found out that it was their private toilet.

Pointing to the notice, I said to Father, "They were here yesterday, not always for their own achievement but mostly because of their long line of ancestors. Is that right?"

Father explained, saying that the peers' families had, over the centuries, supported or sometimes rebelled against royalty.

"It doesn't matter any more which side they were on, but then they had influence and power," he said.

"And now their descendants are still considered special people?" I asked.

"Yes, my dear," said Father. "They are and will be, as long as we have royalty, and that will be forever."

We went back into the Abbey for a last look, to smell the perfume from the flowers, and to hear the organ still playing to the glory of God and the Queen.

Afterwards, we walked across Parliament Square, up Whitehall, and to The Mall. The crowds were even tighter packed, and Father took Frieda's arm and my arm and held them tightly against him.

"I mustn't lose you two," he said.

Poor Brenda was left to trail behind us, but she never complained.

The decorations and flags were up in The Mall, flying and showing off their damp but bright colours in the cold wind. We walked all the way to Buckingham Palace – or as close as we could get, with all the crowds gathered. There were people in their thousands and tens of thousands – perhaps even more – all waiting, hoping, and straining their attention towards the balcony. They were shouting, "We want the Queen! We want the Queen!"

At last, their wish was granted. She appeared on the balcony and waved her hand. The cheering grew louder and louder, until it echoed back from the distant buildings. Such enthusiasm is contagious, and before we realised what we were doing, we too were waving our arms in the air and shouting "God save the Queen" over and over again. For a moment, I felt as if she were also my queen.

"Fantastic. It was fantastic," Frieda and I said after the Queen had gone inside again.

"We were lucky," said Father. "I'd hoped and prayed for a lucky day. Now we have literally been to London to see the Queen. Don't you agree, Brenda?"

"Yes, it was lovely," she murmured, and I could see from her eyes that she was enjoying the day as much as we were.

Nobody seemed to be in a hurry to go home, and nor were we. But it was getting dark and Father said we had a long walk before we could catch a bus. So we left Buckingham Palace, all lit up.

Father again held our arms tight against his lean body – so hard that our arms ached – and we started to walk back. The wind was now against us and his long wet gabardine raincoat was flapping against our stockinged legs. Very occasionally he glanced behind to see if Brenda was still there.

We pushed through the crowds towards Trafalgar Square. Somewhere in The Strand we caught a bus to our hotel and supper. We were very hungry, and the roast pork and vegetables tasted delicious.

"Hunger makes food taste twice as good, and today I feel like the Queen having her coronation dinner," I said to Brenda.

I slept like a log, until 5 o'clock when I was woken by dustmen with their noisy dustcart outside my window. Perhaps the Queen had the same experience. There must have been dozens of dustcarts in The Mall clearing up the mess.

After breakfast, followed by souvenir shopping, we took the train back home. In Birmingham again, we thanked Father and Brenda for all their kindness, and jumped onto our bus.

At home, we thanked Mrs Dixon for allowing us such a memorable day, and we gave her a little souvenir from the coronation. Even a week later, we thought we'd never stop talking about what we'd seen and done. But soon we had a new interest – Klaudia.

Frieda was naturally excited about Klaudia's arrival because the two had been friends at school. Frieda had cleaned and polished her room, and put flowers in a vase for her. Mr Knight had been sent to the station, and when we heard the car coming up the drive, we rushed to the door.

Frieda took Klaudia to meet Mrs Dixon, and I went to make the tea. Frieda then brought Klaudia down to our sitting room, for her first cup of English tea, just as I had experienced it.

Klaudia was a strong-looking, friendly girl. She smiled a lot and her blue eyes were lively. She spoke English with a stronger accent than Frieda. Klaudia came from Freiburg and had never been away from home before.

"I'm so happy to be here. Leaving home wasn't as bad as I thought," she told us. "My father was terribly strict, and never, never allowed me to go anywhere, not even with my girl friend."

Turning to Frieda, she said, "You must remember, Frieda, how I cried. I have never had a boyfriend. I don't even know any boys, except my cousins. I used to go to the cinema with my mother, and my father didn't even like that. I had to come straight back from school, and college, too." She concluded, sorrowfully: "I don't know if I like going out now."

"In that case," I told her, "you've come to the right place because you won't have any temptations to escape."

"It was Frieda, of course, who wrote to my father about this place," Klaudia told us. "I wanted to come here, so at last my father wrote to Mrs Dixon. She must have told him how she cared for her girls, because only then was I allowed to come and join Frieda."

"I'm glad I wrote to your father," said Frieda. "It was the best thing for you to leave home and go far away from your father. Here, you don't need to go anywhere, except the English class with me. You'll like it and you'll meet lots of German girls there."

"I'd better get used to this freedom," said Klaudia.

She was a homely girl – what else could she be? At first, she felt terribly homesick. We all tried to cheer her up, and eventually we succeeded. She stopped talking about home and started to be interested in "Tennessee" and its people. She didn't have an enquiring mind like Frieda, though, and often escaped to her own room.

The weather was still very cold when she arrived, and it stayed that way for more than a week. One evening, I had to go to Klaudia's room to get a book. I knocked on the door and then opened it very slowly. It was so hot in her room; it was just like going into a sauna.

Klaudia was lying on her bed, in a thin nightie, looking at some photographs.

"Klaudia!" I gasped. "How did you get this room so hot?"

Looking around, I saw her window.

"How did you think of that?" I asked her.

What I'd seen was an eiderdown that Klaudia had nailed into the window frame. Another eiderdown was on her bed, on top of the one that had originally been put there. Then I noticed that the gas fire was full on, along with an electric fire that was also turned up to maximum and which she must have found somewhere in the house.

"Klaudia, how can you stand this heat?" I asked.

She hesitated, and then said she didn't like the cold.

"But it is much too hot," I told her. "It must be nearly 40 degrees in here. And it's dangerous for you."

"Perhaps," replied Klaudia, calmly, before adding, "I keep the fires on all night, too."

After that, Frieda and I no longer wondered why Klaudia went to her room so early in the evenings. All the same, we were worried that she might have an accident with both fires burning and so many eiderdowns close to them in that small room.

Somehow, I never liked to go to her room again, in case she thought I was spying on her.

But then the weather changed, and summer arrived.

Chapter 12

The Scottish holiday idea had taken root with us – so much so that we had now planned it and asked Klaudia if she would take care of Mrs Dixon for a week or so.

"I'm very happy to be here alone," she told us. "I wouldn't like to go to Scotland at all."

Klaudia had learned more of our tricks and was perfectly capable of taking care of Mrs Dixon and herself.

Mrs Dixon was very reluctant, at first, to let us go for such a long time, but after Mrs Meyer told her how safe it was in youth hostels and how we two girls would look after each other, she finally gave her blessing to our expedition.

"Well Mrs Meyer, if you say so, but I wouldn't like anything to happen to my girls," she said.

We bought our return ticket to Kendal, and from there we planned to hitch-hike to Scotland, but we kept that a secret from Mrs Dixon.

We packed our walking clothes. I'd brought a pair of trousers with me from Finland, but I'd never dared wear them at "Tennessee". We packed good walking shoes, jumpers and, of course, waterproof anoraks. I'd always imagined that such clothes wouldn't be necessary in a temperate climate like England.

"You'll certainly need them – you're going to Scotland!" Mrs Meyer told us. "It's still in the Ice Age," she joked.

She had loaned us lots of camping equipment, and briefed us about the route, buses and youth hostels. She was just as enthusiastic about the trip as we were. We were a little frightened about hitch-hiking, but she said that Scotland was a very safe place.

On the evening before our departure, we said our goodbyes to Mrs Dixon, as we planned to leave very early the next morning.

We giggled with excitement all the way to the train station. The journey was interesting. I love travelling and never get bored because there is always so much to see: the industrial towns that look so miserable on a rainy day; the sweet little villages; the hills and fields. I was enthralled.

We ate our sandwiches and fruit for lunch and from Kendal took a bus straight to Windermere. Finally, we arrived in Ambleside, where we stopped at a youth hostel for the night. We'd done well so far, and after a good meal we slept like logs.

Next morning, we were up bright and early. After breakfast, we were sorting out our rucksacks in the bright sunshine in front of the hostel when suddenly someone came up to us from behind and put a hand on my shoulder. It was Lukas!

"Good heavens," I gasped in complete amazement. "Are you on holiday too?" I asked him.

"I came especially to see you," he told us as we gazed in surprise at him. "Isn't that a good enough reason to be here?" he asked, smiling at us. "Actually," he added, "it was my mother who gave me the hint. She thought you may need some protection."

"That's very kind of you," I said, eventually. "I don't know that we'll need protection but we're glad you came."

Could I see a moment's disappointment, or perhaps jealousy, on Frieda's face? Whether I did or not, Lukas had to play it fair and safe and be a gentleman for both of us, as he had the knowledge and experience of the places and walks we had planned. Eventually, we were very glad he'd come to join us.

When we learned that a group of people was planning to climb Helvellyn, we asked if we could join the expedition. First, we took our rucksacks to another youth hostel and then, after an early lunch, we began the climb.

It was a completely new experience for me, as we didn't have such mountains in Finland. We had a long walk along the ridge – but when we were halfway there, it started to rain. At first, the rain was fine but towards the end it was coming down heavily. We were so wet that, despite our anoraks, we were soaked through to the skin. Luckily, we kept warm from walking and didn't feel cold.

Back at the hostel, in the changing room and showers, I realised that colour from my red jumper had run not only into all my other clothes but had stained my skin as well. I was red all over.

It was as well we had that to laugh about, because we had been close to despair at the end of such a wet day. Lukas had tried to console us by saying that we would feel wonderful in the morning and all our clothes would be dry.

The next day, we felt the effects of the Helvellyn climb – our backs and legs were very sore – but we had many miles to walk that day. Fortunately, the weather had changed and was sunny, and it stayed that way for the rest of our two days in the Lake District.

We walked for miles and miles, coming down into the valleys at night-time. We carried our lunches in our rucksacks and stopped on the sunny and sheltered slopes to enjoy our sausages, eggs, bread and milk.

At last we came to Ullswater, which looked strikingly beautiful in the sunshine. However, when the sun went behind a dark cloud, it looked quite frightening.

Lukas left us there, and we were truly grateful that he had joined us and guided us through the lonely countryside.

We continued our journey to Scotland, via Carlisle, travelling partly by bus and partly by hitchhiking. We had no trouble hitching lifts. Once, we thumbed a ride in the back of a small, slow lorry.

From Glasgow, we just had to go and see Loch Lomond which, with heavy clouds looming over it, looked very sombre and mysterious. Walking from there to

Stirling, we were given a lift without even asking. It was only in a tractor and trailer, but it stopped for us and in the trailer stood a most handsome Scotsman wearing a kilt.

The journey wasn't very long but it was very slow. The Scot, of course, wanted to know where we came from and where we were heading. For a change, we could understand him very well, so we chatted busily all the way through the village.

We inspected Stirling Castle, which Robert the Bruce was still guarding, and finally came to Edinburgh youth hostel just in time for high tea.

It was the last night of our holiday, so we joined a few young people from the hostel as they went for a pub crawl. According to Mrs Dixon's standards, this was sinning, but it made the evening even more exciting to remember her with affection.

"You know," said Frieda, "this is my first time in a pub."

I said that I had learnt this sin in London.

"I think it's my turn to buy the beer," I said to her.

I collected the glasses and carried them through to the bar. I put the glasses on the counter and looked around. I saw all the men looking at me, and then they started to shout at me.

"Out! Out of here! What are you doing in here?" they demanded.

I turned towards them and said, "I'm having these glasses filled. That's all."

"Oh no you're not!" they shouted at me.

"Yes I am," I replied, defiantly. "Why not?" I asked.

"Don't you know that women aren't allowed in here?" they shouted.

"Why not?" I asked again.

A long explanation followed, which I couldn't really understand. But I didn't really care because the barman came to fill my glasses, saying, "I can see that you're a foreigner, but for the sake of peace, please don't come in again."

"No – I wouldn't give you the pleasure," I retorted.

As a Scandinavian, I couldn't understand such segregation, and I told others how they treated women as second-class citizens in Scotland. For the people in the bar, I suppose it was something to laugh about.

The sun was setting as we returned to the hostel. It was now full of people, and the room where we had our beds contained at least a dozen people in various stages of preparing for a good night's sleep. It had been a hot day and the room was warm. The last rays of the sun were streaming straight at us through the large, bare windows.

In the bed next to me, a young woman with long reddish hair and a long flannelette nightdress had just put a hot water bottle into her bed.

"She'll be melting," I whispered to Frieda.

In the middle of all the bustle and noise, the woman calmly knelt beside her bed, put her hands together, buried her head in her arms, and loudly said a long prayer. Everyone stopped and stared at her, and then just carried on with what they had been doing.

Next morning, we were up early and had time to see Holyrood House, John Knox's house, and the beautiful Princes Street. Then we dashed to the station to catch our train back home. We were back at "Tennessee" in time for a late supper.

While Mrs Dixon was washing her eggs, we had a long story to tell her about our lovely holiday. Getting to know the country by travelling is an experience no books can describe. Even Mrs Dixon was now glad that we had made an effort to see some of her beautiful country.

"I prayed every evening for your safety and I was heard," she told us.

At the beginning of summer, Mrs Dixon's missionary meetings started, and then continued every Saturday afternoon right through until autumn.

The tea-house at the bottom of the garden had been cleaned by Villis and his assistant. The cream and green painted walls were dusted free of the winter's cobwebs; the curtains, windows and their green frames were washed free of dead flies; and the tables and benches were arranged in long rows on the bare tiled floor.

While the cleaning made it look better, there was still the dreary air of the workhouse about the place.

We girls were intrigued about the whole missionary idea.

"My dears, you can come along to the meetings," said Mrs Dixon. "Mr Norman is going to speak about missionary work in Africa, and then we'll have tea."

She told us a long story about Mr Norman and his family, and their years of missionary work in various parts of the world.

Mrs Allen told us what would happen at the meeting.

"We have four old women helpers," she said. "They come regularly to make the cheese rolls for tea. They serve it and then clean the place afterwards. Mrs Dixon has invited me to the meeting, and I'll bring my daughter Stella with me. It will be terribly boring for her but she'll enjoy the tea."

On Saturday morning, the group of old ladies arrived, with their bags full of bridge rolls, margarine, cheese, biscuits, tea and sugar. The milk had been delivered and Villis had already stored it away.

We girls went to see what was happening in the tea-house. We saw the helpers grating the cheese and mixing it with water; the resulting paste was put on the cut rolls that were thinly spread with margarine. The filled rolls were piled high on oval meat plates.

The ladies had also brought white tablecloths – they looked more like old sheets but they brightened up the tea-house enormously. The thick cups and saucers were arranged on a side table, ready for the thirsty crowd.

After a quick lunch, Mrs Dixon went upstairs to dress. Mrs Allen had warned us that Mrs Dixon usually wore a most dreadful hat, but even so, we could hardly keep a straight face when we saw her coming down the stairs in a faded pink dress and an old straw hat covered with tattered silk flowers. Of course, we told her that she looked very pretty, but Mrs Dixon hardly noticed us – she was busily adjusting a hat-pin.

Today was an important day for her, and she asked us, a little nervously, if we were ready.

"If you are, follow me after a couple of minutes, and sit somewhere at the back of the room."

She picked up her stick and went out through the garden door.

Villis had opened the large gates at lunchtime, and soon afterwards people had started coming in, strolling around the garden before the meeting began. A few latecomers were hurrying to the tea-house, and as they passed Mrs Dixon, she slowed down to let them find their seats before she entered the room. We followed behind her.

The weather was glorious and the garden looked beautiful. We certainly had God's blessing. We found seats in the last row, next to Mrs Allen and her daughter. There were a few empty seats, so there would be plenty of rolls and biscuits for everyone.

The talk was quite interesting, but I wondered if these mostly elderly people in the audience were really aware of the hazards involved in missionary work in deepest Africa. Could anyone even imagine that, a few years later, these same mission-trained Africans would adopt Marxist doctrines, arm themselves with AK47 rifles, and butcher those same white people who had made it their lives' work to better the tribesmen's lives?

Perhaps their main reason for being at the meeting was to have a nice outing and an afternoon tea.

Did it really matter anyway? The important thing to Mrs Dixon was to spread the gospel. She also looked forward to her traditional meetings with these same people week after week, year after year.

Chapter 13

The summer also brought us its real highlight – the Pocket Testament League (PTL) annual meeting.

The PTL had been started by Mrs Dixon and her first husband. The aim was to get everyone to carry a small New Testament in their pocket and to read it whenever they had a moment to spare.

This summer, the weather was perfect, so the meeting was going to be held in the garden.

Villis and his assistant had arranged all the benches and chairs on the lawn. Higher up, where the lawn made a terrace, there was a row of the best chairs for the president of the PTL – who was, naturally, Mrs Dixon – and the chairman, officers and speakers.

The guests – the men all in their dark, sombre suits and the ladies in their garden-party hats – started to arrive soon after lunch. They walked in the garden, enjoying its beauty and seclusion.

In the meantime, Mrs Dixon was putting the finishing touches to her old flowery dress, and to another even more flowery hat.

"I'd like you girls to change quickly and come to the meeting," Mrs Dixon told us when she came downstairs. "You know the PTL is very important and precious to us. It was our baby."

When everyone was seated, Mrs Dixon walked to her seat on the lawn terrace, to the sound of applause and greetings. She sat down.

After the chairman's opening address, she struggled to her feet to welcome everyone. She was supposed to say only a few words, but, true to her nature, she went on and on and on.

At last, the speaker had the chance to talk about the league's work in different parts of the world. He'd hardly started to talk when Mrs Dixon fell asleep. Her head fell forward and the tattered flowers on her hat drooped further over her face. Sometimes we could hear faint snoring noises.

At the end of the meeting, Mr Alexander's hymns woke her up. She didn't look at all apologetic, but quickly and enthusiastically joined in the singing.

Mrs Allen told us this happened every year and the members were quite used to it. More importantly, she was a perfect hostess, and after the meeting she talked to all the members in the tea-room.

The tea was good – this time, we had not only cakes but fish paste rolls, too.

Among the 17 weekly helpers who used to come to the house was a Mrs Roberts. She was a chiropodist but had given up her practice when she got married. The only person she still looked after was Mrs Dixon, who was also godmother to Mrs Roberts's daughter.

In late spring, Mrs Roberts had acquired a new au pair girl – a Finn called Leena. I was asked to go and meet her, so one day I walked to Mrs Roberts's house, which was not far from us.

Leena was nearly my age, blonde, and lively. We soon became friends and I often walked there in the afternoons to see her. Leena once came to meet Mrs Dixon, who liked her. We always had a lot to talk and laugh about, as we shared our experiences. I learned a lot about her household that Mrs Dixon, thank goodness, had no knowledge of.

We could never have guessed what Mrs Roberts was really like when she came to visit us at Tennessee, in her grey Sunbeam car, looking pale and without any make-up. In reality, she was anything but plain.

On the contrary, she was a very nice, jolly and sophisticated woman with an interesting life. Her house was large and tastefully furnished with antiques. Her husband was a big and placid man, with a kind face. He owned a sausage factory and left early every morning for work. As Mrs Roberts apparently went into the kitchen only very rarely, her husband – with Leena's help – cooked the evening meal.

"Today," Leena told me one afternoon, "you will meet Dr K. He comes here every morning after Mr Roberts has gone to work. He is her lover."

I was amazed.

"How do you know?" I asked her, before begging her to tell me more.

"I suppose I can but only if you can keep a secret," Leena told me.

She relayed the whole story and I've never even whispered it to anyone.

"One morning," Leena told me, "before I was used to the household routine, I heard the front door opening. I jumped out of bed and ran to the landing. I was just about to go down the stairs when I saw Mrs Roberts going down, naked, to greet Dr K, who had just come in with his own key.

"Luckily they didn't see me. I froze, and crept back to bed to recover from the shock. From then on, I've stayed in my room until I've heard movement downstairs."

"Poor things," I said, innocently. "I wonder if there's something wrong with their marriage."

Actually, Dr K was a true friend of the family. He was in the house most evenings, and the three of them always went out together.

When I was there one afternoon, the doctor was again at the Roberts's house. They were going to have a party for their friends. When Mrs Roberts arrived home and saw me, she suggested that I stay for the party, and sleep at the house overnight.

"You're very welcome to join us," she told me.

I thanked her but said I couldn't possibly stay.

"Nonsense," said Mrs Roberts, "of course you can. I'll ring Mrs Dixon and tell her that you'll be keeping Leena company as we shall be away. She can't refuse."

So she rang Mrs Dixon's number. She had to wait a long while for Mrs Dixon to answer, then had to give a lengthy explanation before getting consent for me to stay.

"Now that's all organised," said Mrs Roberts, putting an arm around my shoulder, "you can relax and enjoy the party with us."

Laughing, Mrs Roberts told her guests about her success in securing my company for the evening, and talked to them about Tennessee and its strict life and regulations. I was standing next to her, smiling and nodding my head.

"We must celebrate this," said Mrs Roberts. "What would you like to drink?"

"Oh, anything alcoholic," I said, then added, "or only slightly alcoholic as I'm not used to it any more."

I helped Leena serve the food, and laughed with happiness all evening at the simple freedom of being at the party. The food was the house speciality – sausages.

After the party, Leena and I cleared up, and happily washed the dishes. I wasn't at all tired, and searched the bottles in case they contained a few drops for my nightcap. I had been energised by the real coffee that had been served – the Roberts didn't have Camp Coffee, which was all we knew at Tennessee.

I talked long into the night about English people, their sophistication and eccentricities, which were so much the opposite of Finns who try to behave in a dull, formal manner – unless they're drunk, in which case they have no manners.

Next morning, early, I walked home through the wild park, at the side of the botanical gardens. The grass was rough near the busy little stream, and the mist still lingered where the sun's rays had yet to penetrate. I jumped lightly over the stream, landing straight in the mud between the tufts of wet grass. I didn't mind anything that morning – the birds were singing as happily as I was, the sky was blue, and the sun was warm on my back.

"We heard from Mrs Dixon that you were on duty all night," the girls said on my return to Tennessee.

"It was good to have different duties for a change," I said. "I'll tell you all about it but first I must go and see Mrs Dixon."

I found her struggling with her sticks outside the nursery.

"Good morning Mrs Dixon," I said, taking her arm and escorting her to the breakfast table. "Thank you so much for letting me stay with Leena."

"It was wise of Mrs Roberts to ring me last night," said Mrs Dixon, "so poor Leena didn't have to be left alone in the house. Our dear God has looked after our darling children and thou art safely home again. It was good of you to stay there with her."

After my unexpected evening of freedom, I could face our puritan life again, knowing that there was, after all, a different kind of world outside this house.

The summer was still warm and glorious, and the garden gave me endless pleasure with its varieties of roses, lilies and climbing plants. It was so much more exotic than anything I was used to in Finland. Even the birds were bigger and fatter here in England. The sunken garden was now overgrown and dry, though still pleasant enough to escape to with a book or to play with Villis's cats. The spring flowers had gone long ago, but there was still interesting and colourful foliage to enjoy.

The heat gave Mrs Allen problems. With her weight to carry, she puffed up and down the stairs, and the morning's house-cleaning efforts were too much for her. She had to sit down every five minutes to rest.

It was even worse for her now as we had extra work – we were expecting visitors, and the guest room had to be cleaned, aired and made ready for them.

We were lucky to have a vacuum cleaner in the house, and although it was an antique, it still worked well enough to get rid of the moth larvae from the carpets.

Once the windows were cleaned, polish applied to the chest of drawers and dressing table, clean tablecloths found in the linen room, and the faded pink quilt put on the freshly-made bed, the room looked very habitable. I picked a bunch of roses from the garden for our visitor, Mrs Dixon's elder sister from Suffolk.

Mr Knight had been sent to collect her from the station, and he duly arrived with this widowed lady, hurrying round to open the car door for her. She was tall, straight and very strict looking. Wearing a beige suit, brown hat and gloves, she looked very "county".

Dotty was at the door with us, organising us to carry her small cases to her room. Dotty then escorted her to Mrs Dixon's study, went and unpacked the cases and put the visitor's clothes away, while we took tea to the nursery for the sisters.

We could very soon see that she wasn't Mrs Dixon's favourite sister, unlike the younger one who was married to a Dutchman and lived in Holland – Mrs Dixon talked about her constantly.

This elder sister came as a stranger, and stayed as such during the few days she was with us. She hardly said anything to us, except to ask our names. "She's not used to foreigners, of course – there are probably no such things in Suffolk," we decided between us.

She was no problem to us or to Mrs Dixon. She didn't even disturb the Saturday missionary meeting. And eventually Mr Knight delivered her back to the train.

When the other sister arrived a couple of weeks later, Mrs Dixon seemed much happier. This sister was small and lively, she had no airs and graces, and she looked as though she'd lived a healthy outdoor life. We even heard the sisters talking and laughing, enjoying a long lunch or tea.

She often came to see us in our sitting room, asking about our English studies or what we were going to have for lunch, as an excuse for spending time with us. She seemed genuinely delighted that we were looking after her sister so well. She stayed for longer than the elder sister, and her husband joined her for the latter part of her stay.

Soon after, their daughter arrived with her new husband. She had obviously inherited her father's Dutch looks. She was a big, heavy woman and her husband matched her in size.

Mrs Dixon seemed ill at ease about her marriage and tried to tell us how sad she had been before. Mrs Dixon never said that her niece had been divorced but we read between the lines. The word "divorce", of course, was taboo in this house.

The couple spent their time sightseeing and meeting friends, and then left to continue their holiday in Scotland.

Mrs Dixon, like the visitors, was relieved with their departure. The couple had obviously felt it wasn't a happy and carefree holiday – more like a duty visit than a real pleasure. There were no late nights, not even for visitors.

For Mrs Meyer, and for us, it had been a busy time. Although there were no extra meals or fuss about the food, we had been asked to produce larger quantities when there was a man in the house.

Chapter 14

Summer holidays were approaching for us, too.

Mrs Meyer and her family went to Vienna, and Mrs Allen stayed on to cook our lunch. She didn't mind at all – indeed, she enjoyed it and often brought her 12-year-old daughter with her for lunch. She was a tall and pretty girl, and was good company for us.

One morning, Mrs Allen arrived laughing loudly and uncontrollably. She collapsed onto a kitchen chair, and laughed while tears streamed down her face.

"What on earth has happened?" we asked her. "Please do tell us," we urged her, several times.

"No, no," she finally gasped, "you won't understand." Frieda and I assured her that we'd try. At last she agreed.

"It started yesterday morning," she told us, subduing her laughter. "My friend Joan and I were in the bus coming here. Next to us was David, our neighbour, who keeps chickens. David told us that the hens were laying well but the cockerel was ill and he was worried about it."

Mrs Allen had to stop her story to burst out laughing again. Struggling to control herself, she continued, "Today, Joan and I were in the bus again, standing, when we saw David at the other end. Joan whispered to me, 'Watch this'. Then she shouted across the bus: 'Hello David, how's your poor cock this morning?'"

Again, Mrs Allen couldn't stop her laughter, and it took a while before she could continue.

"Poor David was standing there, blushing, and not knowing where to look as everyone's eyes were fixed on him. We could hardly hear the noise of the bus for people's laughter."

Mrs Allen had to stop again, trying to control herself.

"David finally had enough courage to shout back, 'Thank God, it's much better today'.

Everyone was having hysterics when he got off at the next stop."

Bewildered, we asked Mrs Allen to explain, so she had the task of telling us about the double meaning so we could share the joke.

I had a stroke of luck one afternoon, when I had gone to see Leena again, this time to help as the Roberts had summer visitors from Holland.

The visitors wanted to know how to get to Stratford-upon-Avon by car, so they could go to the theatre. We showed them the route on the map, but they were afraid they might not find the right roads so they asked if one of us would go with them.

What a chance, I thought, and as neither Leena nor the rest of the family could spare the time, I said I'd ask Mrs Dixon if I could go.

It took me a long while to explain to Mrs Dixon that Shakespeare was nearly as important to me as the Bible. At last she agreed.

"Well, if you can guide them to Stratford, to help poor Mrs Roberts, I suppose you can go," she said.

Thanking her, I reminded her that it wasn't long since Frieda and I had been in Stratford, so I remembered it well.

I rang Leena straight away, and next day I heard that the visitors had bought an extra theatre ticket and were coming to fetch me early, to be in time for the matinee performance.

We found our way easily, and even had time to stop in Henley-in-Arden, which was very pretty and had lots of old English inns.

"Perhaps this is an old staging post," I said, showing off my knowledge of English life.

We chose an interesting-looking old inn, the Bird In Hand.

"This is my very first visit to a country pub," I said, looking at the dark walls and polished horse brasses.

After the Dutch visitors had drunk their beer and I'd had my orange juice, I watched as the barman casually dipped my glass into the washing-up bowl that was full of dirty brown water and then put it to dry on the draining board. I was horrified, but felt so protective of the English way of life that I tried to hide the scene from the Dutch visitors. I also remembered, from my school days, that the Dutch were so clean they even washed the outside of their houses.

The production of Hamlet at the theatre was wonderful. I thought I knew a little about the play, but I still found it difficult to understand. The Dutch visitors agreed, and said that Shakespearean language was difficult even for English people to understand. I didn't mind, though, as it was superbly acted and produced.

I wondered if the foreigners in the audience really liked Shakespeare, or if they just pretended to enjoy it, like a long Wagner opera. All the same, it was a lovely day for us and we enjoyed the play to the end.

"Poor girls," I thought, thinking of my friends at Tennessee. "They will be green with envy this time."

We girls continued to go to our weekly English classes, and enjoyed meeting our friends for coffee afterwards. Frieda and Klaudia had their German friends, and I had Leena and Tiina, my Finnish friends.

One evening, Tiina was nearly crying as she told us about her toothache and how her dentist wanted to take out four of her lovely teeth and replace them with a plate. We, too, were horrified and urged her to find another dentist.

"How can you go home with false teeth? You're far too young for that," we told her. "After all, isn't it a dentist's job to keep teeth in rather than take them out?"

With the help of the family she was staying with, she found another, younger, dentist who filled her teeth beautifully and saved her from the English fashion of having false teeth.

The bus trips to town weren't as hazardous as we'd been told by Mrs Dixon. They were our only way of seeing the outside world – our educational trips into the unknown.

It must have been on a bus that I picked up some fleas, and I noticed them only when I was washing my underwear in the bathroom. There, before my eyes, was a flea in the water among my panties.

"Frieda!" I called. "Come and see if you can recognise this insect."

She announced, with certainty, that it was a flea.

"That's what I thought," I told her, "and I don't like them at all."

"How did it come here?" asked Frieda.

"I suppose it found me on the bus and liked me," I joked.

It wasn't my fault that there was a flea in my wash, but it made me feel dirty and slovenly. The real shock came next morning when I was woken up by an itch on my leg. I jumped out of bed and was horrified to see fleas on my sheet. I quickly covered them with the other sheet and blanket, rolled them up and took them out into the garden. There I shook them vigorously and left them on the bench in the sun.

I didn't find the incident as funny as Frieda did, until later when I asked her to help me take the mattress into the garden as well.

"I don't know what else I can do," I said, remembering that, in Finland, my bedclothes were put on the balcony nearly every week, even in winter, to be aired.

Frieda agreed with me, but Mrs Allen threw up her hands in horror.

"Don't be so silly," she said.

"We can do it," I told her.

"Well mind Mrs Dixon doesn't see you – she'd have a fit," Mrs Allen warned.

"We'll be very quiet," I told her. "In fact, we won't disturb Mrs Dixon any more than we'll disturb the fleas," I joked.

But it wasn't so easy. The mattress was heavy and stiff, and the staircase was narrow with bends in it. I was heaving the mattress from the lower end, while Frieda was trying to hold it up from the top.

"Mein Gott! You are crazy, really crazy," she kept saying. By that stage, we were laughing so much we could hardly move, and the quieter we tried to be, the more we laughed.

Finally, we got the mattress to the garden bench, where I beat it and brushed it carefully, working right under the buttons and into the folds. There were no fleas in sight. Perhaps they'd enjoyed the bus journey more than the bumpy ride down the stairs to the garden, and had got off quickly.

To make sure they weren't hiding in my bedroom, I cleaned that thoroughly, too, washing the floor as well as the bed. Daris came to help me heave the mattress back upstairs, which turned out to be an even more difficult and hilarious task. Klaudia had to come to push Frieda, who was pushing the mattress, to help me drag it up.

"I know why these fleas like me so much," I told them, as we heaved and pushed. "I haven't even seen a sauna for months. We Finns have such trust in a sauna, that even a daily shower can't make up for it."

Later, Mrs Meyer told us it was quite common to catch fleas on a bus.

"Even if you do, it's not the end of the world," she assured me.

One day, Mrs Dixon surprised us by telling us about her annual Bank Holiday outing for all her current and former workers. The outing was due to take place the following week.

"We're going to Malvern," she told us, "to a house called Wynds Point, where Jenny Lind once lived but which now belongs to our family."

We looked at her in surprised delight.

"We always go there but this time we'll have our darling girls with us," she said.

From now on, Mrs Dixon used every spare moment to tell us who was coming on the outing and what kind of position they'd had in the household. Unfortunately, there weren't many of the old retainers left, but with current employees and their spouses, we could easily fill a coach.

The day before the outing, loaves of bread, margarine, cheese, Spam, eggs, salads and biscuits were delivered to the house. Mrs Allen – who was in charge of the lunch and tea – came with her daughter to pack the food into baskets.

At 9 o'clock on the day, the coach arrived, already with a number of smiling and happy old faces at the windows. We carried the baskets and boxes into the coach, and then helped Mrs Dixon to climb on board, one pushing her from behind and Frieda and me pulling her arms.

She gave a gracious wave of greeting to everyone on the coach, then settled down in the front seat. Miss Brown, who was left behind to look after the house, was standing by the door waving her white handkerchief as the coach slowly drove away.

We hadn't gone far when Mrs Dixon's head started to droop and she slept contentedly all the way to Malvern.

The day was gloriously sunny, but windy. The countryside had changed since Frieda and I were there in the spring. Most of the harvesting had been done, but some fields were still green with rows of sugar beet and vegetables. The fruit trees were heavy with produce. It all looked so peaceful and prosperous.

Klaudia, who hadn't been far outside the "prison" of Tennessee, was delighted with it all.

"It's much nicer than I thought," she told us. "There are no factories and tall chimneys to spoil the countryside."

The Malvern Hills were a majestic sight. The coach climbed up the narrow road from the valley, past the small, enchanting town of Malvern, still higher to Wynds Point.

The house was like a large Victorian cottage, surrounded by terraced lawns and tall trees. The upstairs bedrooms had white-painted balconies, and wide French doors led to the sunny garden. Most of the outside walls were covered with flowering climbers. It looked very romantic, and somehow very comfortable too.

As soon as we stopped, Mrs Allen rushed to the kitchen to make cups of tea. Someone found a sheltered place for Mrs Dixon on the garden terrace, where we were going to have our picnic lunch.

Everybody was eager to stretch their legs after the long coach journey, and came to help us unpack the lunch. The place suddenly became alive with people strolling around, inspecting the flowers or trying to recognise distant landmarks.

After our plain but healthy lunch, Mrs Dixon – who had been chatting to her visitors – turned to us and insisted that we walk to the British Camp.

"What is that?" we asked her.

"Well, it's something to do with soldiers during a war," she answered, vaguely.

We decided it might be worthy of inspection.

It was getting colder and windier as we climber higher up the hillside, and we saw black clouds gathering over the summit ahead of us. The lonely hillside with the racing dark clouds made me think of Wuthering Heights.

At the end of a long walk, we came to the site of the British Camp. Now it was just earthworks for the original Iron Age hill fort, but the views were wonderful.

In the twilight of the evening, on the return coach journey, there were many tired and drooping heads.

Frieda and I thought our own holiday trip had been more exciting, but this was the old folks' one and only annual holiday, and it was over for another year.

Chapter 15

One late summer evening, when Leena and I were having a quick cup of coffee in town with some other Finnish girls, after our English lesson, Leena suddenly said, "Girls, do you know that there's a dance at the university tonight? Let's all go!"

Tiina's eyes opened wide. "Yes, do let's. I've been there before and it's fun," she said excitedly.

I looked sadly at these "free" girls, and told them, "I'd love to come but you know I can't. It's impossible. It's awful."

But Leena insisted.

"Of course you can come, at least for a while, and does it really matter if you're late for once?" she said.

"Yes, it does matter," I told her, "and the risk isn't worth it."

But Leena went on, "At least come to see the place. It's only just past nine o'clock. You have plenty of time."

I turned to Frieda and Klaudia, to see if they were interested. Frieda was against the idea, and Klaudia was doubtful because she'd never been to a dance, and if Frieda didn't want to go, Klaudia wouldn't even try to see what it was all about.

"Frieda," I said at last. "I think I'll go, just for 20 minutes. I'll be home before 10. Please tell Mrs Dixon that I'm still talking to Leena but will follow you on the next bus."

Frieda agreed.

We left hurriedly, and on the bus to the university, I told Leena. "I'm worried, but I know what I must do. The first man who asks me to dance can take me home. I'll ask him."

Leena laughed, and said, "Let's hope you'll be so lucky, and that he has a car."

"More importantly," I sighed, "let's hope someone asks me to dance. It's a long walk home to Tennessee otherwise."

I was cheered as we came in sight of the university, because the car park was full. The hall was also packed with people.

The pungent haze of cigarette smoke, perspiration and stale perfume made the air so thick we could hardly see to the other end of the room. We found some empty chairs by the front door and sat down behind a wall of people who were standing with their backs to us, chatting and laughing.

Slowly, a man in front of me turned around and muttered something that sounded like, "Come and have a dance."

I was up like a shot. There wasn't any room to move, thank goodness, so I had a chance to talk to him.

"Are you a student here?" I asked him.

"Good heavens no!" he replied in surprise. "I left this place years ago. You can see what age has done to me."

He stroked his nearly bald head. Of course, one couldn't help but notice it, but I was trying to be polite.

Having noticed my accent, he asked where I came from.

"Finland," he said, when I told him.

"That's very interesting. What's your name?"

I told him, and he said his name was Simon.

Straight away, I said, "Simon, I have a problem. Can I ask you to take me home straight away, please? It's important. You do have a car, don't you?"

"What are you saying?" he asked. "I can't hear a thing."

I stopped dancing and repeated my request in his ear.

"Yes, I have a car but what's the hurry?" he asked.

"I'll tell you later, in the car. I would be eternally grateful if you could drive me home now. It's only to Moseley," I pleaded.

"Now?" asked Simon in disbelief.

"Yes now, please," I implored him.

"In that case, we'll leave at once," he said.

He took my hand and I followed him through the crowds. I had no time to say anything to the girls, who were probably dancing anyway.

I took a quick look at Simon, hoping he'd be all right to drive because he smelt as if he'd had a few pints of beer. I told myself that even if he was a bit tipsy, his blue eyes were very kind and he had taken me seriously.

"The car is somewhere here," he said, as I followed him, row after row, looking for it. Just as I was starting to panic, he spotted it in the middle of the car park. It was an open-top sports car.

"Can you get out of here?" I asked him, anxiously.

"Trust Simon," he said. "You worry too much."

The cars had been parked so badly that he had to try a couple of routes before finding a way out.

"I live in Moseley, in Moor Green Lane," I told him. "I know the place," he said. "It's very posh."

"Yes, I know it is," I agreed. "I help an old lady there and she is very strict. I have to be home by 10 o'clock."

"But she's not so strict that I can't telephone you some time?" asked Simon.

"No, you can't do that. It isn't allowed at all," I told him. "But I'd like to see you again. How can I contact you?" he asked.

We were nearing Tennessee, so in a hurry, I said, "If you go back to the hall, you'll see my Finnish friends sitting by the door, on the right-hand side. The very blonde one is Leena. Go and talk to her. She's very nice."

"Right, I'll go and wake up the sleeping princess," said Simon, as we came to the gates.

"Thank you Simon. You can drop me here. Many thanks. You've been a wonderful help."

I jumped out of the car, and ran to the door, turning to wave to Simon.

I was home in time. The girls weren't very impressed with my luck, nor I with the dance as I'd not had enough time to enjoy it.

I'd nearly forgotten the whole incident, until I saw Leena the following week. Simon had gone back to the university, found Leena and danced with her the whole evening. After that, it didn't take long for him to fall head over heels in love with her. She grew very fond of Simon, too, and their friendship lasted long after Leena had gone back to Finland.

There was never any question of marriage, as Simon would never have tied himself down with anyone, and he is still a happy bachelor. But he changed Leena's life, because he had many friends and together they enjoyed parties, picnics, and pub crawls in the country. I never had a chance to go with them, but I enjoyed hearing about their outings.

One morning, some weeks after the dance, the phone rang as I was dusting the booth under the stairs. I picked up the earpiece and heard Leena's voice.

"Kaisu, I have great news," she told me. "You've been invited to a house-warming party being given by a friend of Simon's."

"What is that?" I asked, not knowing what such a party was.

"The friends have bought a house with a big garden," Leena explained, "and this is their first party there. It's on Saturday at 8.30 and they'd like you to come. So will you go and ask Mrs Dixon's permission? I'll arrange for someone to pick you up."

"How lovely, Leena," I said. "Will you wait, while I go and ask her now?"

Knowing Mrs Dixon, Leena was prepared to wait. I ran to the nursery where Mrs Dixon was having her breakfast.

"Mrs Dixon," I said, with trepidation. "Leena has phoned and is now waiting for an answer. She's been invited to her friends' house-warming party. Can I go, please?"

"It's very nice of her to ask you too," said Mrs Dixon. "She's a very pleasant girl and I know Mrs Roberts takes such good care of her. I'm wondering, though, what sort of friends they are, who have invited both of you?"

I started to get a little impatient. "They're a young couple, professional people. They're all right," I told her, trying to help her decide.

"But you've not met them," said Mrs Dixon.

"No, but Leena knows them well."

"Perhaps, in this case, we can trust Leena's judgment," Mrs Dixon said.

"I believe Mrs Roberts has met Leena's friends," I said, trying to hurry her up.

"Of course, if Mrs Roberts says they're good people, then perhaps you, my darling, can go with Leena and enjoy it, as long as you're home by 10 o'clock.

"By 10?" I nearly shouted. "I can't possibly come home so soon from a party. It doesn't leave me any time to talk to anybody, and the party starts late, because people have to work in the daytime."

I could feel my frustration building up.

"My dear child," said Mrs Dixon, calm as calm. "I'm your English mother and I'm responsible for you. I can't let my children get into trouble, and in any case no-one in this house has ever stayed out at a party after 10.

"Darling, it's the only decent way to live. God would never forgive me if I left any of my children to stray in the streets, as some mothers do.

"My child, I've seen many bad things happening, even in daytime, when I've been around the world, and what happens in the darkness is beyond comprehension."

I thought she'd never stop. She was defending her case as if the whole world outside the house was her enemy. In desperation, I said, "But I'm not going into the streets. I'm going to a family party. I've not been to a party to meet people in the whole time I've been here. Now I have a chance to see a little bit of English family life. They have two small sons, so it can't be bad to visit such people."

I wasn't quite truthful about wanting to meet people, but it was near enough.

"Please let me stay longer, Mrs Dixon, just this once. I would enjoy it so much," I pleaded, urgently, knowing that Leena was still hanging on the other end of the line.

"But I'm very worried about how you'll get home so late. Do you know if these people will bring you home?" worried Mrs Dixon.

"Yes, I do know," I said. "Leena has arranged everything. Some friends of the family are fetching us and bringing us home again."

Did I detect a note of desperation in my voice?

"Well," said Mrs Dixon, slowly. "If you're quite sure."

I was beginning to hope, and rudely interrupted her, saying, "Yes, I'm quite sure. No harm will come to me if I stay longer."

"You make it very difficult for me," said Mrs Dixon. "But perhaps I could let you stay – until 11 o'clock."

The verdict surprised and disappointed me, so much that I nearly cried.

"What?" I exploded. "Only until 11 o'clock? I'm not going at all then. That's it. If I can't stay until 12 o'clock, them I'm not going at all."

I was angry now, and quite cheeky.

I didn't mind, though, and felt that Mrs Dixon sometimes liked someone to stand up to her. She enjoyed the challenge of an argument.

111

She looked at me calmly, though her cheeks were getting more colour and a small pink blotch had appeared on her neck.

"My dear child," she continued. "I am your English mother, and I am responsible for you. How can I possibly agree to that kind of thing? The party can't go on that long. They have to work, and for that they have to have a good night's sleep."

"I do agree with you," I said, "and that's why the party is on Saturday evening, so they can rest on Sunday. We, too, rest on Sunday."

I was nearly in tears.

"Well, it gives me great pain, but if you promise that you'll never say anything about this to the other girls, perhaps I can make this one exception," said Mrs Dixon, finally.

"I know the girls will be in bed, but of course I can't even think of getting any rest until you're safely home and back in my care. Perhaps I could let you stay until 12 o'clock. Oh, it hurts me even to say it. Do you realise that is midnight and that all God's children should be in bed by then? Nobody has ever stayed out so late in this house."

At last she stopped, and looked at me with defeat in her eyes. I had caused it and felt ashamed, but I was also relieved that the battle was now over.

"Yes," I said, quietly. "I do realise that it's midnight. I won't say a word to the other girls. Thank you for letting me stay out longer. Thank you so much."

I tried not to sound too happy, and concentrated on appearing responsible. Hurriedly, I put my arm around Mrs Dixon's shoulders and kissed her hot cheek.

"I must go and tell Leena," I said. "She's still waiting on the phone, I hope."

Mrs Dixon's head dropped forward, and she said, "Look, my egg has gone quite cold."

I ran downstairs faster than I'd ever done before in that house. Leena was still hanging on.

"Where on earth have you been all this time?" she asked. "Arguing with Mrs Dixon," I told her. "I mustn't say anything to anybody, but I can stay until 12 o'clock."

"Lovely. Good for you," said Leena. "I'll arrange for someone to come to the house at eight o'clock to fetch you."

"I can't wait until Saturday," I sighed.

"It's going to be a big party," said Leena. "I must go now, though. I'll see you there."

I thanked her for inviting me.

"It was Simon and his friends who invited us," she said. "They're jolly nice people."

I sat there in that little telephone box for a long time, weary of the battle I'd won. I marvelled at the thought that I'd be the first person in this house to stay out until midnight, and at a party, too.

Poor Mrs Dixon. She'd gone through such agony. It can't have been easy for her to have an au pair girl, and I vowed not to let her down.

Of course, I had to tell the girls that I was going out with Leena, but I didn't mention my homecoming and luckily they didn't ask.

My next few days were spent in happy anticipation, wondering about Saturday, thinking about what to wear, and wondering who, and in what car, would come to collect me.

On Saturday morning, Leena rang me.

"Trevor, a friend of Simon's, seems to be the only one without a girlfriend. He'll pick you up," Leena told me.

"Don't forget to ask him to wait for me behind the hedge," I reminded her. "I'll be ready by eight o'clock."

In fact, I was ready at 7.30. I was wearing my best turquoise dress, and had my hair curled. Frieda and Klaudia were also excited about my party, but even in their wildest dreams they couldn't imagine a late night. I'd told them only that Mrs Dixon was going to let me in.

The girls were in our sitting room, reading, when I went in to show myself to them.

"You look all right in that dress," they said.

"That's good, because I must go and get Mrs Dixon's approval now," I told them.

I found her in the study.

"Thank you for letting me go," I said to her. "I'm ready now and will be back as promised."

"My dear child," she began. "I've also promised myself that I won't worry about you, but of course I will. Now, let's have a look at you."

She examined me closely.

"You look very pretty in that dress, but I think it's a bit too open at the neck," she told me.

"Is it?" I asked in astonishment. "I think it's all right," I added.

"My dear, what you need is a modesty vest. I have some nice ones here in the bedroom, I think."

Without taking any notice of my protests, she hobbled to a large chest of drawers. I didn't dare to say anything else in case she stopped me going altogether.

I knew that my dress was very sober looking. It was made of fine wool, and had a V neck and a pleated skirt. For Mrs Dixon, though, that neck opening was too low.

In the drawer, she found a few modesty vests from which she chose one that was once white. It was now discoloured with age but I could still see delicate embroidery on it. Finding a couple of safety pins, she fixed the modesty vest inside my dress, nearly up to my throat.

"It looks better now," she said. "All nice girls wore these inside V necks. You can keep this one. I have more of them. Now, have a good time. I will wait for you. Are you sure that somebody will bring you home?"

"Yes," I reassured her. "Goodbye and thank you again."

I felt like a real Victorian maiden, nearly curtsying to her in my gratitude, and dressed up to her virginal standards, pale and uninteresting without any make-up.

I had already planned to do something about that, though, and ran back up to my room. The old lipstick still worked, as did the mascara, and at last I was ready to enjoy my evening.

Chapter 16

Quietly, I crept downstairs, with my coat and handbag on my arm. I didn't want anyone to come and see me off.

I ran out to the street and stopped behind the hedge. There was no flashy car waiting for me – only a motorbike with a bearded man standing beside it. He walked towards me.

"Hello," he said. "My name is Trevor. I assume you're Kaisu. I've come to fetch you."

"Thank you. That's very kind of you," I replied, putting on my coat and climbing onto the pillion.

"Sorry about my taxi," Trevor said. "It's not very posh but we'll get there. I hope you didn't expect a limousine. I'm not that rich yet," he said, laughing.

"This will be a new experience for me," I told him.

"Hold on tightly to me. The tighter the better," he said, as we roared off down the road but not so fast that I was frightened. The streets were quiet, with hardly any traffic, and the evening was calm and warm – a perfect party evening.

I was still clinging onto Trevor's waist when we drove in through gates that bore a sign saying The Red House. Trevor stopped the bike beside a strong-looking man who turned and smiled, showing off his handsome face and large white teeth.

"Hello," he said. "Now, let's get you off that horrible bike," and he lifted me high, as if I were a child. Trevor introduced us.

"This is your host, James, and this is your Finnish guest, Kaisu."

As James set me down on the ground, he said, "Leena has told me all about you. You know, we nearly had a bet about whether you'd be able to join us at all. I'm glad you managed it. Come and meet Alice, my wife, and the other guests."

He led me into a large hall, where there was a punchbowl on the table, with glasses and cocktail food. James introduced me to Alice and gave me a glass of punch, saying, "I suppose you haven't had this kind of drink for a long time. Don't forget to come for a fill-up when your glass is empty."

Alice was very slim and beautiful, but she seemed very cold and distant. She took me to meet some of the other guests.

I stood with my glass in my hand, answering questions about my life in England and what I thought about it. But as I did so, I was listening in amazement to the way in which people were talking so lightly and jokingly about different subjects. What a change from the atmosphere at Tennessee.

One day, I decided, my English will be nearly as good as that, but for now I was content just to listen. The conversations were so quick that often, when I'd understood a light-hearted comment and wanted to join in, the subject had changed before I could translate in my mind what I wanted to say.

Leena took me out to see the garden where – now it was dark – the trees were lit with coloured fairy lights. On the balustrade of the terrace, there were swedes with faces carved out of them and candles inside.

Simon came over to us, smiled, and hugged me as if he'd known me forever.

"You know," he told me, "you gave me the best advice I've ever had. 'Go back to the dance and meet Leena', you told me, and look at me now – getting more bald and tamed and suffering the pains of love. I got my reward for taking you home."

"It was my lucky day, too," I told him, "otherwise I wouldn't be here now."

Trevor joined us, and told me about the friendship between himself, James and Simon, which had lasted through childhood, school and university, and was still going strong.

"We tolerate each other," he joked. "We blow up sometimes, as you can do only in a loving family. But tell us about your family here. It sounds as if you're living in a Quaker convent or a prison," he said.

"I'm not sorry for myself," I told him. "I'm a voluntary prisoner. It's all been a new experience for me – a trip back in history. In a few months, I shall be back in Helsinki," and freedom, I thought to myself.

Would I still know what to do with it, though? I'd be responsible for myself again, and my life would be of my own making. I was lucky – I had work waiting for me there – but would my experience here in England open more doors for me in Helsinki? I was excited to find out.

Alice and James were excellent hosts, the latter being naturally full of fun. At the buffet table, he introduced me to his boss, Andrew. He wasn't as tall as James or as handsome, but in his dark suit and stiff white collar, he looked well groomed and he stood proudly.

He bowed slightly to me. "How do you do?" he said. "I've heard about James's Finnish friends."

He asked how I spelled my name – I was used to this, but I was always surprised at people's reactions to meeting a Finn.

"You must tell me about Finland," said Andrew. "I'm afraid I don't know much about it."

We had supper together, sitting on the sofa, and completely forgot the party that was going on merrily around us.

Andrew asked about my work in Finland and England, and about my family and my hobbies. I imagined he was talking to me like the lawyer he was, with confidence in his manner and precision in his voice. He had a serious look in

118

his blue eyes, and a wide forehead where his thick and tidy dark brown hair had a slight wave.

He offered me a cigarette. I hesitated.

"I haven't had a cigarette for a long time, but I'm going to risk it and hope that I don't faint," I said.

"No, please don't," said Andrew. "I'm not very good at nursing fallen ladies."

His face changed as he laughed, and his prominent nose looked much smaller. To a Finn, who is used only to small noses, any standard-sized nose is a big one.

I thought he was good looking; he was just below six feet tall, neither slim nor fat, and he was very formal – very much a lawyer – although he also had a good sense of humour.

Like me, he was in his late 20s. He told me that he was the youngest in his family, and both his older sisters were married. He had joined the Navy during the war, rising to the rank of naval lieutenant, and had then gone on to read law at Cambridge University.

By far the most important achievement so far in his life was to start his own law firm, which he'd done about 18 months before. It had been a struggle, but he was proud and confident about the business's future. James – our host – had failed his law exam and been Andrew's managing clerk from the beginning.

I soon realised that Andrew was an ambitious man, and a hard worker, and that he wanted to become a politician.

"Before I get there, though, I must establish myself," he said.

"At the moment, I live with my mother and father, as a matter of convenience. I have converted part of their home, which is an old vicarage, into a second office. It's a good idea to expand into the suburbs. It's a struggle to become known, which is why it's useful to belong to different associations."

Andrew was speaking eagerly and enthusiastically, seemingly with plans to conquer the world. I told him that I was just existing, but with a purpose – my battle would start when I returned to the rat-race of Helsinki.

We had been completely absorbed in our conversation, when I suddenly realised we were alone in the room.

"They're playing hide and seek somewhere, I suppose," said Andrew. "Shall we join them for a while? Though I'd rather sit here and talk to you."

From the laughter, I judged it was a jolly party.

"It's nearly midnight, and I must go home," I told Andrew.

"I'll take you home," he said, "but I think you should ring Mrs Dixon and tell her that everyone here wants you to stay longer."

Andrew insisted, and James said the same, with others joining in, so soon we were dialling Mrs Dixon's number. I tried again and again, while listening to everyone's ideas for the excuse I would give her, but there was no answer.

"Tell her the car has broken down," or "the tyre is flat", or "tell her anything so that you can stay," came the advice.

But Mrs Dixon, being slightly deaf, couldn't hear the phone ringing so didn't have to listen to my lies.

"That's easy. You've tried ringing her. You'll never get another chance in that house to go to a party, so why not stay now, while you can?" Andrew said, persuasively.

"You must forget Mrs Dixon and enjoy the party. I will take you home and will explain why you stayed later. Trust me," he said.

I was close to tears, but at last he convinced me and I forgot the time. The temptation had been too strong. I felt guilty, but not for long.

"Come and have a drink," said Andrew. "You need it now, and please don't worry or you'll spoil the party for yourself."

120

I decided not to look at the clock. The music was louder and the floor was clearing for dancing. In the middle of the room, while I concentrated on Andrew's one, two, three, steps, Mrs Dixon's anxious face started to fade from my mind. He applied the same one, two, three rhythm to all dances.

"Actually, it isn't quite right for an Englishman to dance properly," Andrew said, to my surprise.

"Really? Why not?" I asked.

"It's thought to be a bit sissy. All you have to know is a couple of basic steps. It works very well."

And indeed, it did work quite well. I liked dancing, and he had a good sense of rhythm, and I heard him humming one of the tunes in a nice baritone voice.

The punch bowl had long since been emptied, and the candles inside the swedes were burning out, but there was still plenty of coffee, liqueurs, jokes and laughter.

Suddenly, I noticed the clock and, in a flash, I woke up to reality. It was half past two. I started to panic.

"Please Andrew, I must go home straight away. I really must," I pleaded, "otherwise Mrs Dixon will call the police or the ambulance, and she doesn't know where I am."

I was desperate, and nearly in tears at the thought of her anxiety. I felt wicked, guilty and panic-stricken. I had betrayed the trust she'd put in me.

At once, Andrew offered to help.

"Of course I'll take you home, but please don't worry. It's not worth it. You're spoiling your lovely time here. It's been wonderful. Just remember that."

I suppose it must have been amusing to the other guests to see an adult so worried about a late night, but then they'd never met Mrs Dixon. I found my coat and hurriedly said my thanks and goodbyes.

In his car, Andrew kept trying to calm me down with promises of explanations, while I cried quietly.

"Please don't cry," he said, softly. "I'll talk to her and she'll understand. You'll see. It will be all right." He squeezed my hand.

A few minutes later, we drove through the gates of Tennessee. The house was in complete darkness and the whole world around us was still. Only our steps on the gravel to the front door made a noise.

I rang the bell, and we waited a long time, in silence. Then I saw the light come on in the nursery.

The window opened, and there was Mrs Dixon leaning out, her white hair curled up for the night, and wearing a dressing gown with large purple flowers on it. She obviously had difficulty locating us in the darkness.

"Is that Kaisu?" we heard her ask, and we could hear the concern in her voice.

"Yes," I called back, timidly. The window closed, and after a long wait we heard the kitchen door opening.

"Don't worry. I'll explain it all to her," Andrew whispered.

Mrs Dixon's worried face appeared at the doorway. She looked angry, and then I saw her sighing with relief.

"Thank God you're safe," she said, before we had a chance to say anything. Without pausing, she continued, "I've been praying for you all night. I've been worried about you but as I didn't know where you were, I couldn't do anything.

"You poor child. How can you be so late? But I can guess. Here is someone who has kept you, though thank God he's brought you safely home.

"But I must say, young man, it's not to your credit to keep these young foreign girls all night at your parties. I know what goes on in these kind of situations, and it's always these innocent ones who suffer.

"I can see from your face, and your wicked eyes, that you try to lead these poor little creatures along the wrong path. I can't do anything, but God in heaven will punish

122

you. You must ask for salvation from your sins so that your guilty conscience isn't so heavy.

"This child has been given to me for a year, and I am her English mother, so I feel guilty, too, that I have let her go to a sinful party that has lasted all night. I'm responsible for my girls and I don't want you or anyone to hurt them.

"You, an Englishman, should have had more sense than to cause so much grief to my Kaisu and me, and I can see from your wicked eyes what you have had in mind."

She didn't stop for a long while, angrily saying the same thing over and over again. She didn't give me a chance to introduce Andrew and what was worse, Andrew had no chance to say anything in his defence. We just stood there and looked at her while she preached at us.

Then, quite suddenly, she stopped. She put her hand on my shoulder, pulled me inside, and banged the door shut, leaving Andrew standing outside.

I stood there, absolutely amazed at her strength.

"So sorry. I'm so sorry about this," was all I could say, looking at the floor.

"And you've been drinking!" I heard her say, angrily, behind me. I turned to look at her and lied, "No, we only had some tea and coffee."

"Go to your bed NOW!" she said, in a frightening voice that I'd never heard before.

"Good night," I whispered, relieved that there wasn't going to be any more discussion about the matter. I quickly crept upstairs to my room, afraid she would call me back again.

Luckily, I hadn't woken the other girls, so they had no idea what time I came home. I stood still inside my door and heard Mrs Dixon going to her room.

I undressed slowly, thinking how utterly wicked I must be in her eyes. I felt guilty but, at the same time, I was glad that I'd done what I'd done. I had no regrets there.

But I felt sorry for Andrew. He'd had no chance to give his brave explanations. But was there really any need for explanations? I supposed there was, just to tell her that the world wasn't as bad as she imagined.

Eventually, I fell asleep, with Andrew very much on my mind.

Chapter 17

Frieda came to wake me up the next morning, when she took Mrs Dixon her early morning cup of tea. Mrs Dixon didn't mention me to her.

When I told the girls about my late night, they weren't surprised, although they thought I was wicked, terribly naughty, and daring.

The atmosphere became worse when Mrs Dixon told Frieda that she wanted to have her Sunday lunch alone, without us girls, in the dining room. Nor were we invited to have the usual Sunday tea with her and Miss E. She didn't want to see me.

"It's the dog kennel for me now. Don't you think this is all so funny?" I asked the girls, pleading for sympathy.

"We wouldn't do it," they answered.

I tried to look as if I didn't care what they thought, and at times I even burst into a nervous giggle. But I didn't cry.

The girls were good enough to take Mrs Dixon's lunch and tea in to her, to save pain on both sides. We thought that's what she would have wanted, although she didn't actually say so.

In the late afternoon, the girls went up to their rooms to rest and read before supper. By then, I was so tired I feared I'd fall asleep, so I went for a long walk in the garden, avoiding the part of the house from which Mrs Dixon might see me.

By the evening, I thought it odd that Mrs Dixon hadn't reminded me of my bad behaviour. Then at 10 o'clock, just as I thought I might go to bed, our sitting room door opened and Mrs Dixon's serious face looked in.

"Kaisu, will you come up to the pantry?" she said, sternly.

I jumped to my feet and followed her without a word.

There were no chairs in the pantry, so we stood facing each other. She was leaning against the cupboard and I was in the middle of the room, looking into her eyes.

"Now," she said. "Tell me – who were these people that you visited last night?" She had a pen and a piece of paper in her hand, and she half turned towards the cupboard so she could write.

"I don't know," I whispered.

"You don't know?" she nearly shouted, her voice high pitched and trembling.

"I'm sorry," I said, "but I don't know. Of course, I heard their surname, but it was an English name and I'm afraid I've forgotten it."

"I see," she said. "Then tell me where they live."

"I'm afraid I don't know that either," I confessed. "I was taken there and brought back, so I've no idea where I've been."

She paused and shook her head, worry in her eyes.

"You poor child. I knew it. I knew it," she said. "You probably don't know it – that there are people who take poor foreign girls out, and even to their homes, and harm them and use them. I shouldn't ever have let you go. We must thank God that you're safely back home."

I tried to reassure her.

"I'm all right, Mrs Dixon, really. It wasn't that kind of place. It was a home."

But she wouldn't hear of it.

"You don't know what happens in those sort of places, where they take poor foreign girls for a visit. I've been a street missionary in many towns, even abroad. I've seen the worst of human nature in action."

She paused, looking at me.

"You look surprised," she said. "Yes! Horrible things happen, in Egypt and other Middle Eastern countries. I've seen it with my own eyes."

I wanted to say that we were in England, but I had no chance as she told me, at length, about her experiences many decades ago. I believed her, because the white slave trade and prostitution were still happening in some countries.

After a long lecture, during which she repeated herself several times, she put her arm around my shoulder and said, "Do you really know what happens in these kind of places?"

I shook my head.

"Well, I'll tell you," she said, looking at me very seriously. "They take you to a house, and do you know what happens then?" I shook my head. "They give you a cup of tea."

There was a long pause, while we looked at each other.

"And do you know what happens then?" she eventually asked.

"No," I said, my eyes wide as I waited to hear what she was going to tell me.

"You fall asleep. And do you know what happens then?"

"No," I said, still wide-eyed.

"You wake up in bed with a man! That's what happens to you," she said, triumphantly.

"Oh no. Nothing like that happened to me," I said.

I didn't dare smile, although I wanted to. I wanted to joke and say that I hadn't been so lucky, but for Mrs Dixon this was very serious.

"I can assure you that it wasn't that sort of place and that I'm perfectly all right," I told her. "Nothing happened to me or anyone else there."

"That might be so, but it could be otherwise," she said. "Tell me. Who was this young man who brought you home last night?"

She obviously couldn't bring herself to say "this morning".

Luckily, when we were in his car, Andrew had pushed his card into my hand and I'd slipped it into my handbag without looking at it. I'd remembered it only during the morning. I had it now, in my pocket.

"Here is his card," I said, as I gave it to her. Mrs Dixon studied it for a long time. She read his name, followed by "MA Cantab. Solicitor", and his address.

"Well," she said, slowly. "I see. Perhaps he is all right."

Then she suddenly looked at me again, and said loudly: "No! No! It can't be so. I saw his wicked eyes and I know that he can't have an honest mind.

"My child, you've been saved from an awful experience. I prayed all night that nothing bad would happen to you, and we must thank God that He has looked after you, where I have failed in my duty.

"You'll never see those people again. You'll be safe here, at home, and we'll try to forget this awful experience. The devil has tried us, and God has saved us from falling into his wicked hands."

She became calm. Then I remembered something.

"I left my scarf there. I'd like to get it back."

It was obviously a bad time to say this.

"You must forget the scarf," she told me. "What is a scarf worth when you've been saved from the wicked world? Forget the scarf, because you'll never see it again. Go to bed now and thank God for his protection, always. Goodnight my child."

"Goodnight," I replied, "and I hope you will sleep well too."

She didn't offer her cheek to be kissed.

I left the pantry, closing the door behind me. The girls were already in their rooms, perhaps fast asleep. I would have liked to wake them up and talk to them, but instead I had to analyse the discussion on my own.

I got into bed. I was very tired, but my mind kept replaying my conversation with Mrs Dixon, and then returning to the delightfully wicked evening I'd enjoyed. Eventually, I fell asleep.

In the morning, Mrs Allen heard about my late home-coming. She was shocked, although clearly amused.

"Fancy you doing that!" she exclaimed. "Was she terribly angry?" Her eyes were round as I told her what had happened. "My God, you were naughty," she said, over and over. She also repeated: "She'll get over it."

Mrs Meyer, though, was on my side and thought it wasn't a bad idea to bring new spirit and more life into the house.

"I do hope you're going to meet that young man again," said Mrs Meyer. "He sounds nice, even though he had no courage to stand up to Mrs Dixon. Not many have."

At least it had given us all something more to talk about than Dear Mr Alexander's hymns and the missionary meetings.

I hadn't told anyone that Andrew had promised to phone me, to hear how I'd got on with Mrs Dixon. I'd warned him to ring only in the evening, when Mrs Dixon was at choir practice.

As soon as Mrs Smith had escorted Mrs Dixon to her car, I went upstairs to Miss Brown's office, to talk to her. As I'd guessed, she already knew about my disastrous night out.

"I can see why you stayed such a long time at the party," she told me, kindly. "I wouldn't have done it, but don't let that disturb you. I'm sure you didn't mean to hurt her – just to enjoy yourself, and that is your right. I'm sure you had a lovely time."

I told her that I had. Then I said, "I wonder if I could ask you something now? I need your help. Andrew might phone me – will you please not mention it to Mrs Dixon if you happen to answer the phone?"

"Yes Kaisu," she said, to my relief. "I shan't mention it to her. After all, I don't need to know who rings you, and I've not heard that talking on the phone isn't allowed."

Andrew did ring me that evening. I believe Miss Brown deliberately let me answer the call.

"How are you, Kaisu?" he asked. "I hope you aren't sad any more. How did you get on yesterday?"

I gave him a shortened version of the previous evening's interview, and told him, "All is well now, but she is a funny old lady with funny ideas about life outside this house."

"Don't let her worry you too much," said Andrew. "I wonder if I can come and see you one evening, when she's out? I'll bring your scarf back then, too."

I excitedly agreed, and we fixed the date and time for an evening when Mrs Dixon would be out at choir practice. But I was still worried about it, and decided to make his visit a short one.

I went to tell Miss Brown about it, before I told the girls. She wasn't surprised. On the contrary, I think she expected it.

"That's all right," she said. "He has a right to know what happened to you, as he must have been anxious. Perhaps you'll see that he doesn't stay too long."

I assured her that I would, and thanked her.

Down in the sitting room, I told the girls about Andrew's visit, and made them promise not to breathe a word to anyone.

"So we'll get to see the little devil, shall we?" teased Klaudia.

A long week passed as I waited for his visit. At last, at the agreed time, I heard his car stop in the road outside. I ran to open the front door for him.

"I'm so glad you've come to see me. I have so much to tell you," I said quietly.

Andrew's voice was much firmer. "I'm very glad to see you looking so much happier than last time," he said.

He looked so formal, and every inch a lawyer, in his dark suit and stiff white collar. He straightened himself, as if wanting to look taller, and stepped into the house.

"I've had a busy day at the office and can't stay very long," he said.

"Come into our sitting room and meet the girls. They know all about our late night," I told him.

He squeezed my hand, and said, "I didn't think in that early Sunday morning that I'd ever see you again."

I told him, "I too thought it was the end of everything."

Pausing in the hall, he turned to look at the darkening garden.

"At least you're lucky to live in such a beautiful place," he said.

I told him how much I loved the garden.

The girls were obviously dying to meet Andrew, though they just said "hello" when I introduced him.

"I came to see how you all were after the earthquake we created here," said Andrew. "I'm very sorry about it."

I'd hardly started to tell Andrew about the discussion in the pantry when there was a knock at the door. It opened immediately and Miss Brown appeared.

"Are you all right?" she asked.

I jumped up and introduced Andrew to her. He shook her hand and told her, "I'm not experienced at rescuing maidens in distress but this time no harm has come to this maiden, despite the doubt."

Smiling, Miss Brown said, "I'm sure that doubt will vanish with time," and she left to go back to her room. The girls, too, got up and said they had to go upstairs.

I was left alone with Andrew, and finished telling him my story. He listened, smiled, and shook his head.

"Now I know that you live in an extraordinary house," he said. "You must get out of here occasionally. Perhaps we can go to the cinema some time. I'll try to ring you again one evening."

I told him I'd like that, if only I dared to do it.

"It would have to be instead of my evening class," I said.

Andrew got up to leave.

"I can let you out through the kitchen door," I said.

At the door, he didn't attempt to hold my hand, or shake it, but just stepped out quickly and said, "Don't forget to ring me if you get into trouble again."

"That's good to know," I said, gratefully, "but I'm sure everything's all right now. Thank you for bringing my scarf back."

I hoped that Miss Brown would see him leaving, because the window of the nursery, where she was working, was just above the kitchen. Soon after Andrew had gone, she came in to tell me that he was "a very nice young man".

Over the following weeks, Andrew phoned and sometimes called for a quick visit. Frieda and Klaudia lost their initial shyness and joined us for a cup of Camp Coffee in our sitting room.

A couple of times, in place of my evening class, we went to the cinema. Once, he bought a box of chocolates for me, and I soon found that he loved them even more than I did. The war years in Finland, and the poor times afterwards, had made me forget the taste of such luxuries.

Andrew was always dressed in a smart suit and commanded respect. He was distant and proper, and terribly English. Our conversations were mostly general – about the weather, the film we'd seen, or his work.

I slowly discovered that he hated to show his feelings.

He didn't seem to have close friends or a wild bachelor life. But I felt that he cared for me, and he was always very protective of me, even though he was so aloof. He was so different from my old sporty boyfriends. He was a true English gentleman.

I tried to match his attitude towards me, and never showed any affection. I was shy with him, but as the weeks went by, I slowly but surely began to fall in love with him.

"He is very formal but nice," I told the girls.

"Are you in love?" they teased me.

I shook my head, as though I had no idea what they were talking about. I was far too proud to admit it even to myself, but I was in love for the first time in my life and I suppose I was a little ashamed because I had no idea if he felt the same way about me.

Perhaps the English way of being in love was not to talk about it, I thought.

Chapter 18

The autumn began to creep in. The garden was still beautiful, with the chrysanthemums in all their glorious colours. I escaped there during the afternoons, to think about Andrew.

I didn't see him often enough, but when we met I enjoyed talking to him or listening to him. He talked about his law practice and the difficulties of becoming known when advertising wasn't allowed. The town offered work and the potential to expand his business, but the difficulty was finding the clients.

I became more and more like a trusted friend, sharing his worries even if I couldn't solve them for him. My problems seemed so small compared with his.

The term's first meeting of the university's Bible Society was due to take place at Tennessee one evening in the autumn. It was an after-supper meeting, with tea and biscuits to be served after the talk and discussion.

The society's president, Mr Pope, was a large man with impressive wealth and looks. He arrived early with the speaker, a vicar. The president was an old friend of Mrs Dixon's, and she often talked to us about this good man, who despite being very busy always had time for the well-being of his students.

Soon the house was full of dark-suited and serious-looking young men. Mrs Dixon was busily smiling and greeting them as they streamed into the drawing room, where Villis had placed benches from the tea-house.

Mrs Dixon called us girls and introduced us to Mr Pope and the vicar.

"Here are Frieda and Klaudia, our two German girls, and this is our little Finn, Kaisu," she said. "They have been here for quite a long time now, and their English is becoming more fluent every day.

"I think they should join the meeting. There are some seats left at the back of the room."

We were always ready to explore new ways of learning, so we filed into the room after everyone had taken their seats. Mrs Dixon, Mr Pope and a couple of elderly gentleman were happily settled into comfortable armchairs.

After the introduction, the vicar – a slight man with pale eyes and a clear voice – talked about the evils of the world. Referring to his Bible every now and again, he eventually came to the devil. He said that the arch devil of the century was Hitler. He talked for a long time about Hitler's evil doings when, quite suddenly, Frieda with her eyes full of tears, jumped up and shouted, "I am German, and I'm not going to listen to any more talk like that. It's wrong to call Hitler a devil. He wasn't a devil," and she walked out of the room.

Klaudia dutifully followed her, and after a second's hesitation I trailed behind them. When I turned round at the door, the talk in the drawing room had stopped and every eye was turned towards us. In the hall, Frieda was crying loudly and repeating her complaint. Klaudia backed her up and was in nearly the same state.

Mrs Dixon seemed to be frozen with shock. Mrs Allen hurried along, and joined me in trying to calm the girls down. She had made the evening tea, and now suggested that we all go to the sitting room and have a cup. I escorted Frieda away, with my arm around her shoulders.

After tea and biscuits, she began to calm down. Mrs Allen tied on her little white apron, saying: "Are you going to be all right now? I must go in, as I'm sure they're in need of a calming cup of tea too."

We never talked about Hitler again, although it was obvious the story had gone through the house, as far as Mrs Meyer, the Austrian cook. I'm sure that she, too, felt guilt for the horrific crimes of war.

"You have a depressing lot of people here," Andrew said, one evening while we were standing in the doorway.

I told him that I did get depressed sometimes but that it was important to see other people's point of view.

Then, testing his reaction, I said, "Soon I shall start to think about going home, and this life will be just a memory."

I looked at him, wanting desperately to hear him comment about the fact that we'd have to part. But he said nothing about it.

Instead, he straightened himself and said, as if he'd rehearsed the words, "Do you think you could come with me to Bournemouth for a weekend? Tell Mrs Dixon you've had a letter from your female cousin and want to go and meet her in London. She'll be staying in a respectable hotel and you'll be staying with her. Mrs Dixon can't refuse, by law. You're entitled to some time off. It'll be all right. Just be confident with your request."

"How lovely, Andrew," I said. "I'll do anything to get away for a day or two."

Andrew said he'd find out about trains and hotels, and write to me.

"You'll then have to write a Finnish letter, just in case she wants to see it. We'll drive to Bournemouth in my car. Pack just a few things, and don't worry – it'll be all right. We both need a rest and a change of scene."

I was on top of the world. He must love me now, otherwise he wouldn't be suggesting this. But why doesn't he say so, I wondered, before deciding that it must be the English way.

I had to tell the girls.

"If you promise not to talk to anyone about it, I'll tell you something very exciting," I said to them.

They eagerly agreed.

After I told them, they asked if Andrew and I were going to be engaged. I had no such good news.

"I'm only going to Bournemouth for a weekend," I told them.

"Mein Gott!" exclaimed Klaudia. "My father would never let me go away, just like that. He is so old-fashioned and strict. You're lucky. You have no father."

Frieda felt sure Andrew and I would get engaged.

I told Leena my secret the next day.

"He must love you," she said, "otherwise he wouldn't ask you to go away with him. You'll see I'm right.

"Why can't he be like Simon, though?" she wondered. "He tells me all the time how much he loves me. I'm very fond of him too, but I don't think I'd like to settle here and I don't love him that much."

Leena and Simon had a busy social life and often drove to the country for the weekend.

"At least my English is nearly perfect," she said.

A couple of days later, I plucked up the courage to talk to Mrs Dixon about my "cousin". With a letter in my hand, I stood for some time outside the nursery door, listening more to my loudly-beating heart than to any sounds that indicated she'd finished her breakfast.

I remembered Andrew's words – to be confident – and knocked on the door.

"Mrs Dixon? May I ask you something?" I hoped I didn't sound too excited. "My cousin Sara has come to London with two women friends, and they'd like to see me there next weekend if it's not too difficult for me to get time off. I'd write to her and she'd come to meet me at the station."

I blurted it all out and hated every word of the lies I was telling.

Mrs Dixon swallowed her last drop of tea and turned to me with a look that made me think she was going to swallow me next – or perhaps it was just my guilty conscience.

"I see," she said at last. "Tell me about your cousin. What is she doing in London?"

I told her Sara was just on holiday.

"She is interested in history and old buildings, and so am I, I thought we could explore together," I said.

"What a good idea," said Mrs Dixon. "Is your cousin married?"

"No, she's not. That's why she has the time to London," I told her, trying to sound convincing.

After more questions about the fictitious cousin's work in Helsinki, Mrs Dixon came to the conclusion that it would be safe, and even beneficial, for me to go and meet her in London.

"Thank you so much," I said, gratefully. "It's very kind of you. I'll let you know what train I'll be getting."

I sighed with relief as I closed the door behind me.

What a liar I am, I said to myself. I hoped it was only a white lie and not worth worrying about. As long as I wasn't hurting anyone, it was all right, I told myself, as I pushed away a thought that "I'll pay for it later".

I had permission to go to a hotel, but not with Andrew. If only Mrs Dixon knew what a sinner she was sheltering under her roof. I was confident that, for her, Andrew was in the past – forgotten, unmentionable, and out of our lives. Nobody would even whisper his name within earshot of her, so she wouldn't dream that he was connected in any way with my weekend away.

Andrew came to see me again for a few minutes in the evening, to tell me his plans. He'd decided it was best to leave early on Saturday morning, when Mrs Dixon would be having her bath and wouldn't see me going.

"How lovely to be going away with you," I said to him, unable to hide my enthusiasm.

I hugged him and kissed his cheek as we parted at the door, and I promised to be ready and waiting for him in the street outside.

He smiled and looked a little embarrassed – without turning to look at me, he walked to his car.

"He's so shy, but I love him," I told Frieda. "I'll take my little navy blue dress with me for the evening – the one I've never worn here."

Frieda said: "You're lucky. You like to have a good time and you'll have it now, but I wouldn't have gone."

I tried to convince her. "One day, Frieda, the same thing will happen to you and change your whole life. You'll see."

Frieda looked serious and asked if I really loved Andrew.

"Yes Frieda," I told her. "Yes, I do love him."

Next morning, I told Mrs Dixon what train I was going to take. Raising her eyes from the morning's post, she said, "Don't forget to take some comfortable shoes with you. Sightseeing isn't easy without them. And don't stay out late – good girls don't.

"In any case, you'll soon be tired. I'm glad that there'll be older ladies with your cousin, who know the town."

I assured her that I would be all right.

Early on Saturday morning, I'd packed my walking shoes, a couple of blouses, my blue dress and my nicest nightie. I took the morning cup of tea in to Mrs Dixon in her bedroom, and said goodbye to her.

"Goodbye my child," she said. "Have a nice time and we'll see you back tomorrow evening."

I hurried to my room, changed my blouse and applied the faintest hint of lipstick. I put on my coat, took my small case and handbag, and went downstairs.

Frieda was in the kitchen.

"Say goodbye to the others for me, and have a nice Sunday," I said.

Frieda came out into the street with me, and soon Andrew drove up and stopped in front of us.

Without many words, we drove off as Frieda waved to us. We'd gone quite a few miles before I started to feel relaxed. I felt as if I was in a film and driving away with the loot!

"It's so good of you to come with me," said Andrew. "I've been working so hard and I really need a couple of days' rest, away from my parents.

"Of course, it's very convenient for me to live at home, especially now that I've opened a new office there. Luckily, my parents' house is an old vicarage, so there's plenty of room for us all. And it's in a part of town where I grew up, so finding business there will be easier, I hope.

"As you know," Andrew continued, "I would really like to go into politics, but first I have to have a good income and funds to support me. One can't trust to politics alone to keep you permanently."

I was flattered when he talked to me like a trusted friend, sharing his worries and ambitions.

"It's interesting to hear about your life," I told him. "It seems to be quite a struggle to build your business but you're obviously a very determined and courageous man, so I'm sure you'll succeed."

Andrew agreed. "Yes, it has been a hard slog, but now I'm going to have a little rest from it. I've booked two rooms in the best hotel, and we'll have a good dinner tonight. I'm really looking forward to it. Aren't you?"

He looked at me and smiled.

"Yes," I said. "To me, it will be something truly special. No sausages and mash for me this weekend – how lovely!"

We'd left Birmingham behind and were driving through gently hilly countryside. It looked green and

140

beautiful. The dull day softened the shadows and, as long as the rain kept away, I lapped up the beauty of it all.

We drove through old villages and country towns, where even the smallest houses seemed to be cared for and loved. What a contrast it all was to the slums that I passed on my weekly bus ride into town.

The black-and-white fairytale thatched cottages were charming and reminded me of the illustrations in my childhood books. Could I ever have imagined, then, that such places were real?

It all looked so different from the Finnish countryside, where the villages were much smaller – often, they had only a couple of wooden houses, a post office, shop and school. The larger Finnish villages also had a stone church.

But farmhouses were in the middle of their fields, often far from any neighbours, and there were long stretches of forest with, every so often, a glittering lake that looked calm and inviting and had a sauna at its shore.

Sauna was the essence of a Finnish Saturday evening – like a day of purification in readiness for the holy day of Sunday.

Chapter 19

We stopped for lunch in a quaint old country pub, and soon afterwards arrived in Bournemouth. With its promenade, it looked grand and very much bigger than I'd imagined. Andrew easily found the hotel.

"Have you been here before?" I asked him.

"Yes, once," was the reply, but there was no explanation of the circumstances.

He picked up my little case and his hold-all, and I followed him to the desk where I heard him confidently asking about his booking.

The receptionist was perfect.

"Very well, sir", "No sir", "Yes sir" and then "Boy!". The "boy" appeared, took our luggage, and said, "This way, sir".

We followed him to our rooms, and Andrew tipped him.

"This is a very nice hotel, Andrew," I said. "Just come and have a look at the view. It's gorgeous."

He came to stand beside me, and said, "I'm glad you're happy. Shall we unpack and then go for a long walk along the front? The sea air here is very relaxing. I'll call you in a few minutes' time."

And then he was gone.

I slumped into a soft armchair and said to myself, "Why am I such a coward? Why didn't I hug him and kiss him, when I'm so happy? Perhaps it would frighten him. I was so sure of my love for him but I don't know if I should express it or leave it alone."

I unpacked and was ready when he called. We walked through the entrance hall like an old married couple, bored with each other's company.

There were flowers and plants with fancy leaves set in intricate patterns and perfect formation in the promenade gardens.

The hotels were grand and decorative, built for the wealthy classes of the Victorian era, some even before that. They were still graceful, and busy with older people. Inside their walls, I thought, there must be countless stories of happiness and sorrow. To me, they were a visual joy, well painted and with brass-work gleaming.

"I do hope they never pull these down and build brick boxes in their place," I said to Andrew.

"I hope that, too," he said, "but sometimes it's necessary."

It alarmed me. I was, and still am, concerned about preserving heritage, and although I'm keen on new architecture, I don't want to fill the world with only modern constructions. Houses and other buildings are monuments of the past, as much as other symbols of civilisation.

"Well, if that has to happen," I said, "surely they could at least keep the outside walls and rebuild or renew the inside. Although I'm a Scandinavian, I love and cherish old things. I never tire of looking at old buildings. Ever since I was a little girl, I've loved houses and wanted to be an architect but there was little chance for a girl when all the men naturally got first choice after the war."

Andrew led me into one of the grandest hotels, suggesting we have tea. There were a few old ladies and gentlemen sitting in the lounge. They fitted so well into their surroundings, it looked as if they'd grown old along with the building.

When the waiter had brought us our tea, Andrew said, "Now, you be mother, and I'll teach you how to serve tea in England."

Every Sunday, I'd seen how Mrs Dixon served tea, but I still took his instructions very seriously. After all, the English tea ritual is second only to the Japanese tea ceremony.

Back at our hotel, Andrew said to me at the door of my room, "I'm going to have a little rest now, and then a hot bath. I'll meet you in the bar at seven. Have a good rest."

I was in the bar, punctually, at seven o'clock. Andrew was already there with a drink in his hand. He gave me a quick welcoming smile but didn't really look at me – or if he did, it was without actually seeing me.

I doubt he noticed that I'd curled my hair, my eyes sparkled with happiness, I'd applied mascara and eye shadow, or even that I wore my flattering figure-hugging navy dress. I didn't "look a million dollars" but I knew that I looked all right and it gave me confidence.

"What would you like to drink?" he asked.

"The same as you, please – a gin and tonic," I said, sitting on a bar stool.

"I think you'd better have a sherry. A medium sherry," he said, to my surprise.

"Really? Why?" I asked him.

"It's better for the ladies," he said, briskly.

The sherry arrived and Andrew raised his glass.

"Cheers!" he said. "Did you have a nice little rest?" he asked.

I said that I did. "It's so quiet here, one can't help falling asleep," I added.

Andrew had been smoking, and got out the packet so he could have another one.

"If I promise not to faint, can I have one too, to go with my sherry?" I asked.

"Of course. I'm sorry," said Andrew, offering me one.

I smoked it very carefully, and didn't cough once.

The dining room wasn't full, and we were shown to a nice table. Andrew handed me the menu. We talked about people and their eating habits.

"It's very important in England to eat the proper way and to hold your knife and fork correctly," he told me.

144

"You see how I'm taking my soup – you ladle it backwards into the spoon. And you don't lean over your soup – you sit up as straight as you can."

I told him I'd not seen this done before but would remember his instructions.

"Here in England, one more or less knows one's social class from the way people eat," he said, seriously.

"Really?" I said, in surprise. "The class system is so strong here. There's a long way to go to equality."

This triggered yet another discussion about the social behaviour of the different classes.

We finished our meal and were waiting for coffee and liqueurs. The band was playing quietly at the other end of the dining room. I watched a fat elderly couple dancing cheek to cheek, obviously enjoying themselves.

"Look at them – they can really dance," I said to Andrew.

"In England, you mustn't stare, and you must speak up. It's best to pretend that you've seen nothing at all," he said, to my amazement.

"Yes. Of course. I'll remember this," I said. I didn't at all mind his instructions and vowed to take better notice of what he said, and pretend to be lady-like. After all, this was the "finishing school" of my year in England!

At last, we got up to dance to the music of the band.

"I love dancing," I told Andrew. "I remember you telling me that it's not very appropriate for an Englishman to dance well, even if he enjoys it," I said. "Ladies have to be good dancers, so they can follow the gentlemen. All the same, I think you dance very well. I've enjoyed it."

"In that case, we'll repeat it," said Andrew, as we returned to our table and he ordered another brandy.

"That reminds me of my first May Ball," he told me, and started on a long story about how he was driving to the ball in Cambridge when his car broke down in the middle of nowhere, in the hottest part of the day.

145

Waiting for help, he had nothing to drink but brandy and champagne, apparently having a case of them in the car.

"I was late for the ball, but quite happy!" he concluded.

Andrew was relaxing now, as he reminisced. We were nearly the last people to leave the dining room. At my door, he stopped, kissed me on the cheek, and said, "Good night. It was a lovely evening. You must be quite tired by now. I'll see you in the morning at nine o'clock for breakfast," and then he was gone.

Did I expect to see signs that he loved me? Or a little wild passion? Yes, I did for a moment, but then decided he was shy. In any case, his English behaviour must have been correct.

He was obviously tired and so was I but I still danced the last waltz alone, in my head, humming "Sleep Sweet My Prince, and Good Night To You."

Next morning, I practised – and passed – my test at "being mother" at the breakfast table.

The day was sunny and we decided to go for a long walk along the cliffs and down to the empty beach. The sea was pounding on the shore with its relentless rhythm, glittering in the sunlight.

"Somewhere beyond the horizon, I was there during the war in a convoy," said Andrew. "Every time I look at the sea, I remember it and I'm grateful that I'm here to remember it again. So many of them aren't."

He was standing straight, his feet firmly planted on the ground against the wind, which was so strong it nearly blew me off my feet and pushed my hair up straight.

We walked, hand in hand, up the cliff and down to our hotel for lunch. It was a delicious saddle of lamb – my best Sunday lunch for months.

We drove home via a different route, which was just as beautiful and interesting as the previous day's journey.

"The train has arrived from London," I said, as we approached the suburbs and I thought of Mrs Dixon's expectations that I'd be arriving from the city.

Andrew parked noiselessly in the street behind the hedge outside Tennessee, and got out to open my door.

"Thank you for coming with me," he said, as we stood beside the car. "I hope you feel better for the rest, too."

He held my hand. I kissed him on the cheek and said, "Thank you for taking me with you. It was a lovely weekend. I'll never forget it."

He got back into the car and said, "I hope to see you again soon. I'll phone you."

He drove away.

Back in my room, I tidied myself and went to see Mrs Dixon to tell her I was back home after a very enjoyable weekend. I sounded so convincing that I didn't need to elaborate. I told a little different but very truthful story to the girls, and Frieda was sufficiently interested to say that she would like to visit Bournemouth.

Later, in my own bed, I tried to sum up the weekend's events. Everything had been perfect, and yet? There was something missing – affection certainly and, dare I hope, love?

Andrew phoned later in the week. He wanted to take me to see an exceptionally good film.

"I'd love to see it. I enjoyed the book very much and I'd learn much more by seeing it than going to my English class."

The film was long and Andrew brought me home by car. There was not time to talk, except for Andrew to tell me how much busier his office was becoming and that, of course, was the most important thing in his life.

I gave him a quick peck on the cheek, although I would have loved to kiss him and hug him properly. He was already the most important thing in my own life.

147

That weekend, Mrs Dixon had to go on a rare visit to Norfolk to see her sister, who'd had an operation. Mr Knight took her to the station and was reminded many times to come and collect her in two days' time, when she would return.

We girls were full of joy. Freedom!

"We're going to do something exciting," Klaudia said, looking in the newspaper to see what was going on in town.

Poor Mrs Dixon thought we'd be lonely while she was away.

"It was clever of you, Frieda, to insist that we could manage in the house on our own," I said. "Let's cook something different and have lunch in the garden."

We had plenty of vegetables, so we made Finnish summer soup and German omelette, and had a hilarious lunch in a sheltered but sunny corner of the garden, with Tigger keeping us company.

Frieda and Klaudia decided to go into town that evening, to a concert or the cinema, and I was staying at home. Before that, I wanted to see Leena. I had to talk to someone who would understand my sense of hopelessness.

It was pleasant walking through the park to her house, although it reminded me of my weekend walk in Bournemouth with Andrew. Everything reminded me of him. How could someone love another person as much as I loved him, I asked myself. I was sure he had no idea, and couldn't begin to imagine it. I had to tell Leena how unhappy I was.

"I suppose I'll have to tell him, and if he doesn't propose I'll kill myself," I said to Leena, nearly crying.

"Don't be silly. No man is worth that," she retorted. "You must cheer up. Being in love shouldn't be so miserable and painful. You look dreadful, and you've lost weight," she said, firmly.

"I know I'm not the same carefree girl I was a few weeks ago," I admitted.

148

"Just to cheer you up, I'll come to see you tomorrow afternoon, with a couple of friends."

Seeing the look on my face, she said, "Don't panic. We won't cause any damage in the house. We'll just look at it and hoot with laughter."

That evening, after the girls had left, Andrew phoned. When he heard that I was alone, he said he'd like to come and see me, just for a few minutes, to make sure I was all right.

It was only to Leena that I had confessed my love and been tearful, so now I told myself that if I was still happy to see Andrew, I must also look happy.

He arrived, smiling and looking happier than ever before, and that helped lift my spirits. With a cup of coffee in our sitting room, we talked at length about Bournemouth. I told him the girls were keen to go there, and Andrew promised to find a way very soon.

"I must go home now. The girls will be back soon," said Andrew.

We got up and I followed him out of the sitting room.

Without a word, he took my hand and started to climb the stairs.

"Which is your room?" he asked.

"This one," I said, opening my bedroom door. "But why?"

He didn't answer, just looked into my eyes and kissed me – not passionately but gently – and closed the door behind us as we stepped into my room.

He led me to my bed and kissed me again and again, so I lost all sense of the world around me. There was just him and me, and my overwhelming love for him.

A sense of time slowly returned to the stillness of the evening. Andrew stirred.

"My dear. My darling," he said. "I must go before we're caught."

At the door, he kissed me goodbye and said he'd ring me as he wanted to see me again soon.

After he'd driven away, I stood at the door for a long time, looking at the empty space where his car had been. Were we lovers now? After all, he'd called me "darling" and kissed me. He must love me now, forever, just as I loved him.

Chapter 20

Next day, after Sunday lunch, Leena and Simon and a car load of friends burst into the house.

After a cup of Camp Coffee, they started to explore. We girls followed them sheepishly, but still pointed out the old bits and pieces of interest. There was the old clothes cupboard, the life-size and other portraits of Dear Mr Alexander, and the old records in the landing cupboard, along with the gramophone with its decorative and beautiful brass horn.

Soon, the boys found a box of old triangular tennis racquets and balls. They dressed up in Mrs Dixon's old sporting outfits and fancy clothes, and had an hilarious game of tennis on the lawn.

We had a "tea dance", with Mr Alexander's hymns and other songs blaring out from the brass horn. At the end of our frivolity, someone gave us a good sermon followed by absolution for our unforgiveable sins.

The laughter and fun continued until someone noticed it was opening time at their favourite pub. They left as quickly as they'd arrived.

After we'd recovered from the invasion, we cleared up the mess so there was no trace of our misbehaviour. We were glad they'd been – and gone – without breaking anything. We agreed we'd all had an excellent afternoon.

The girls thought they were funny, wild and friendly, but also typically English. We promised never to tell anyone about the invasion and we never broke that promise. Luckily, there were never any complaints from the neighbours.

After a week, I went back to my state of desperate unhappiness. Even a quick visit from Andrew didn't help much. The upstairs episode wasn't mentioned. I didn't laugh any more, or talk very much. I felt the pain and it showed on my face.

One day, Mrs Dixon stopped me in the hall. She put her arm around my shoulders and looked at me searchingly, before saying, "Kaisu, my darling, are you all right? Thou looks so sad these days. It is because thou art going home soon?"

Thank goodness she'd given me the answer.

"Yes, it's just that, I'm sure," I told her. "I know there's still a long while before that day arrives, but I've had a wonderful time here," I said.

"And thou will have an even more wonderful time at home with your own people and friends. There is no place like home," said Mrs Dixon.

The old cliché really hit me and I thought, "If only I had a home."

And was I going back, alone, with my misery, smiling and waving goodbye to everyone? I must at least pretend that all was well. I must shake myself and face the facts. If it has to be so, then it will be.

A couple of days later, Mrs Dixon was in the kitchen with us as she counted her eggs. She said Mrs Smith had a bad cold and wouldn't be able to take her to the concert.

"It's such a pity," she said, "because this time it will be an especially good one."

Thinking it would help me forget my woes for a while, I offered to go with her.

"Would you really come with me?" she asked. "Thou will enjoy the beautiful Mozart concerto."

I told her I was already looking forward to it.

Next evening, I was ready early, looking pale in my dark coat. When I went to the study, I found Miss Brown hovering around Mrs Dixon, asking if she had her handkerchief in her handbag and if she'd like to wear a warmer dress as the evening was quite cold and windy.

"I'm perfectly all right in this one," Mrs Dixon was telling her. "I trust my helper will get me into the first bus after the concert, so we'll have no time to get cold."

152

Mrs Dixon winked her eye at me and laughed.

I found her sticks, while Miss Brown found her coat, hat and gloves and helped her put them on. Then she followed us to the front door where Mr Knight was dutifully waiting for us, and he helped her into the car.

Sitting in that old Ford was like being in a taxi – high up on the back seat with plenty of leg room for the sticks between us. In front, Mr Knight had his PTL hat on his very round head.

"This is my first live concert in England and I'm really looking forward to it," I told Mrs Dixon.

"Thou will enjoy seeing the orchestra and conductor, because I always sit at the end of the balcony where the view is best," she said.

We arrived at the Town Hall in a slight drizzle. Mr Knight took us to the door, held out an umbrella for us as we joined the crowds, then handed it to me in case it was still raining when we queued for the bus afterwards.

I followed Mrs Dixon's slow progress up to the balcony. There was only one row of very uncomfortable-looking hard and high seats at the end. We were obviously going to occupy two of them. No wonder no-one else was going to sit near us, even though the hall was rapidly filling up.

A wooden floor sloped down from our seats to the solid wooden balcony railing. I propped up our dripping umbrella. I suppose the seats were especially high so one could see the orchestra over the railing. We had no programme, but I'd glanced at the poster downstairs. Mrs Dixon was telling me about her favourite Mozart piece.

At last, the conductor appeared, to welcoming applause. After silence had fallen, his baton went up and beautifully elegant music filled the hall. I closed my eyes occasionally, trying to concentrate on the slow movement.

Quite suddenly, I heard a crash. It was Mrs Dixon's stick, which had fallen from her lap and rolled down the wooden floor to the railing. To my horror, Mrs Dixon had closed her eyes. Worse, she was fast asleep and hadn't even heard her stick crash to the floor. I didn't dare to wake her up, and pretended I hadn't seen or heard anything. At that point, she was still holding her other stick but, just as suddenly, her grip on that one loosened too, and the stick fell to the floor, where it rolled down and hit the umbrella, which also crashed down.

The audience was now visibly annoyed and stared at us angrily. Happily, Mrs Dixon was blissfully unaware, but I was ashamed and lowered my head, looking out at the disgusted people from under my brows. I wanted to apologise to them all but could only sit and be stared at.

Later, Mrs Dixon's handbag also fell to the floor, landing first on the hard metal clasp with a bang. Her snoring went on peacefully until the sound of clapping woke her up.

"That was beautiful, wasn't it? These concerts are always good and I enjoy seeing the conductor's hands," she said, enthusiastically.

The evening had become colder and it was raining harder when we left the hall. Using the umbrella, I tried to keep the wind and rain off our faces, while dirt from the streets splashed onto our shoes and ankles. People in the queue helped me get Mrs Dixon into the bus, and we arrived safely at home.

Later, I told Mrs Smith about our noisy accidents. She calmly said that it had happened before. Others in the house giggled when I related what had happened.

On another cold, wet and windy evening, when Mrs Dixon was out at choir practice, Andrew gave me a quick ring to say he was popping in to see me.

The girls had sought the warmth and peace of their own rooms, to read, and I was alone in the sitting room in front of the small gas fire. Even Miss Brown had left unusually early to go home.

"What a filthy night," Andrew said, as he shook his coat. "I hope your sitting room is warm and cheerful?"

He put his arms around my shoulders and gave me a quick kiss on the lips. Over our coffee, we talked about the events of the week.

I was next to the Welsh dresser, listening to him, when he suddenly got up and came to stand beside me. He looked at me for what seemed a long time, put his hand on mine, and said, "Would you like to marry me? I would so like to marry you. I know we would be very happy."

He straightened himself up and looked at me seriously.

Of course, I was very surprised at first, but then immensely happy. I was very sure of myself when I answered, "I will. Yes, I will marry you. I love you more than I've ever loved anybody."

"Good. That's good," he replied.

I closed my eyes and in my mind repeated his proposal, just to make sure I'd understood him correctly.

"I'm so happy," I whispered.

I opened my eyes and saw his business mood coming on.

"Now," he said. "We must make some arrangements. First of all, I must get you a ring. Secondly, you must come and meet my parents. Thirdly, we must tell Mrs Dixon. Perhaps you'll talk to her at the right opportunity."

I said I'd tell her and the others in the house, and asked if I should wait until he had bought a ring.

"You can decide that yourself. Whatever suits you best," he said. "My mother's leg burn is getting better, and as soon as she's properly up and about, you must come to tea."

Assuming a business-like manner, he continued, "I think we should get married in the spring, after you've been back to Finland."

I agreed.

"I shall have so many things to think about and arrange in Helsinki – my job, my flat, my furniture, my insurance," I said. "But the main thing is that I'm not afraid of the future. On the contrary, I feel that I've arrived," I told him as I squeezed his hand.

"I have every confidence that you'll arrange everything from here," he said. "I can't help you very much. There is so much to talk about but I must go home now. I'm behind with my law reading and I've got a heavy day tomorrow. Good night, my darling. Sleep well and don't worry too much."

I kissed him.

I was still standing in the dark kitchen when I heard Mrs Dixon coming home from choir practice. I mustn't tell her anything yet, I said to myself, not before I've told the girls.

I helped her with the eggs, while she talked about her evening. Nearly an hour later, when she'd kissed me goodnight, I went upstairs and knocked on the girls' doors.

"Frieda, come to Klaudia's room. I have something important to tell you," I said.

Poor Frieda shot to her feet, looking very apprehensive.

In the warmth of Klaudia's room, I excitedly said, "Guess what's happened to me? Something terribly important in my life."

Frieda said: "I suppose Andrew has proposed at last?"

I asked, with surprise, how she knew that was going to happen.

"Well, he needs a wife, and you're in love with him," she said. "I'm glad for you and hope you'll be very happy."

Klaudia joined Frieda with her good wishes, and added, "I'd never marry in England, and nor would Frieda. So you're going to stay here for the rest of your life? Without your old friends? How can you take it so calmly?"

"I suppose it's because I have no home or parents, as you have," I told her. "I already think of this place in quite a different way. It's going to be my home. I know the town isn't attractive, but the country around is beautiful, don't you think? And we'll live somewhere near green fields and tall trees and bright flowers."

We were planning and dreaming of my future until midnight.

"How funny," I mused. "Someone comes and says something, and with a few small words my whole life has changed. For better? For worse? Who knows? It's been quite a day for me."

I kept on thinking of those small words when I was in bed, well wrapped up in my blue pyjamas. I could never have thought that I would have to learn not only to live with, but also to sleep with, a foreigner.

Next day, when we were having lunch, I said to Mrs Meyer, "I have something exciting to tell you, but please don't say anything to anyone until I've told Mrs Dixon."

The girls were there too, waiting with anticipation to see her reaction to the news.

"I'm getting married," I told her.

"Mein Gott!" she exclaimed. "It's Andrew, of course," she added. "How wonderful."

She walked round to my side of the table and hugged me.

"I'm so glad," she said. "I'm sure he's a nice boy and will make you very happy. I've heard so much about him. What wonderful news. Now you'll be staying in Birmingham and we can see each other and be friends."

"I must tell Mrs Dixon, but I'm scared to say anything to her," I confessed. "I'm waiting for the right opportunity, but it'll come."

"Yes it will, but don't worry," said Mrs Meyer, kindly. "Mrs Dixon is old and she's seen a lot of life. She'll understand, even though you may not think so."

Chapter 21

A couple of days later, to my surprise, Andrew came to the house unannounced. I took him to our sitting room, where the girls congratulated him, shaking hands formally with him.

He noticed a Finnish card on the mantelpiece and asked whether it had anything to do with our engagement.

"No," I said. "Today is St Catherine's Day, my name day. In Finland, we celebrate it, especially if we don't want to tell anyone about our birthday and our age."

"Really?" said Andrew.

After a while, he got up.

"I must go now," he said. "Goodnight, ladies."

He took my hand as we got to the kitchen and pushed a ring onto my finger. It was the most beautiful diamond ring I'd seen for a long time.

"Is it the right size?" he asked. "I can change it if it doesn't fit."

I told him that it fitted perfectly.

"It's beautiful and I'll treasure it forever," I said, and kissed him, telling him that I loved him.

"I love you too," he said, at last, and kissed me. "We're now officially engaged to be married. You can tell everyone."

After he'd gone, I rushed back to the sitting room to show the girls my ring.

"I'm not going to wear it until I've told Mrs Dixon," I said.

The opportunity came very soon afterwards, when Mrs Dixon stopped me in the hall. She put her hands on my shoulders, looked at me, and said, "You seem to be better now than you have been lately. I'm glad you feel all right about going home. It won't be long, now, before you're back in Helsinki, my dear child."

159

Now, I thought – I must tell her now. I looked into her eyes and said, "I'm not going home. I'm staying in England."

Mrs Dixon froze, and there was a long silence. Quietly, she said, "Is it that man?"

I nodded, and said "Yes."

We stood there, looking at each other.

Then she said. "I knew it! I knew it! I don't know how but I knew it!"

She nearly shouted the last words, and burst out laughing. Then she became serious again, and with her hand still on my shoulder, turned her piercing gaze on me and said, "My child, I should be very angry with you, but I'm not. Neither am I going to ask you any questions. I'm only very glad for you and hope that you'll be very happy. Now, you must bring him here and we must have an engagement party. I want to meet your beloved properly now."

The good news quickly spread around the house, and Mrs Dixon told everyone who came near her all about my "beloved one". The usual question was, "How did you manage to meet anyone at this convent and get so far with it?"

The only person who never asked anything was Mrs Dixon. She knew I'd been dishonest with her and I hoped she didn't really mind any more. My secret meetings with Andrew were never mentioned.

But it all made her remember her own love affair, with Dear Mr Alexander, and she talked happily about it to us for hours.

"We'll have a party next Sunday, Kaisu dear. Would you ask your beloved one to come for tea then? It'll be a very special tea – our dear one's engagement party," said Mrs Dixon. "I'll ask Mrs Meyer to bring some cakes."

160

Andrew was pleased to accept the invitation, although he looked a little apprehensive when he arrived, punctually at 3.30 on Sunday afternoon.

I took him to the drawing room where Mrs Dixon was already sitting with Miss E, her former secretary. She, as usual, had come to spend the Sunday afternoon with her old "boss".

"Good luck," I whispered to Andrew, taking his hand to lead him in and introduce him properly to the ladies. Then I left the room to help the girls lay the table.

"If he has any charm, he had better turn it on now," said Klaudia.

"Yes, it would help," I said, "but too much of it could ruin everything."

"He isn't that handsome, is he, Frieda?" said Klaudia in her frank way.

"Oh Klaudia. Let's be nice to her. It's her engagement party," said Frieda, laughing.

"Yes," I said, as I put a bowl of roses from the garden into the middle of the dining table, "you can say that sort of thing tomorrow, but not today."

There were plates of sliced bread spread with margarine, and ham – which now, in the colder weather, was looking quite edible – biscuits, cakes and a jar of blackcurrant jam.

At four o'clock, I played the Big Ben chimes extra loudly, and in a few minutes Mrs Dixon was organising our seats at the table. An extra long grace was said, directed at Andrew's and my happiness and blessing our future life. Then Mrs Dixon poured the tea carefully, talking all the time about the coming wedding.

"When did you say, my dear Andrew – or my dear son, as I should now say, of course – that the big day was going to be?" asked Mrs Dixon.

Andrew explained again, saying: "Kaisu will go to Finland first, to arrange her business affairs there, and then we'll get married in March."

"In church, of course," said Mrs Dixon excitedly, "and I'll give her away. After all, I'm her English mother and I think in this case I can also be her English father. It would be my pleasure to give my dear Kaisu to her beloved one in marriage."

That seemed to set the seal on my engagement. I was blissfully happy, and completely relieved from all the anxiety and worry.

What a blessing it was to be ignorant and innocent about things to come. Even the thought of Mrs Dixon giving me away didn't worry me. I trusted that Andrew was capable of sorting it all out.

"My dear son," said Mrs Dixon at the end of the tea party. "I'm sure you and Kaisu have a lot to talk about and plan together, so I think it would be all right to let you go to the nursery for a while. I think 10 minutes is ample, so you can have a good talk."

She turned to me, and said, "Kaisu dear, will you take your beloved upstairs and Frieda will call you when the time is up."

Andrew thanked her, playing his part perfectly and seriously. I tried to smile lovingly, although I really wanted to burst out laughing. Taking his hand, I led him upstairs to the nursery. We closed the door and gave way to our laughter.

"Now you can see what a funny house this is," I said, hugging him.

"It's more than funny – it's priceless," said Andrew.

"Shall we sit down and make faces at each other or do you have a better idea about how to spend 10 minutes?" he asked.

I sat opposite him and suddenly felt shy.

"You see now that I don't live in the real world," I confided. "In fact, I often wonder if I'll be able to face the outside world again. I know I shouldn't be afraid, because I trust that you'll teach me the English way of living. I know I'll be all right. I want to be a perfect wife to you."

Andrew looked at me and said, "I know you'll be all right."

The light was shining on his face, and his blue eyes looked pale and serious. I wish I had been able to detect just a little twinkle in them.

I knew he wasn't very handsome but he seemed reliable – perhaps often tense, too, but likeable and kind, and I was in love with him.

"Well, what else shall we talk about?" I asked, looking at my watch.

A knock at the door put a stop to our time together in the nursery. I heard Frieda's voice saying, "Time's up" followed by a giggle. "Will you come down now?" she asked.

We followed her downstairs, where everyone was waiting for us.

"Ah, here you are my dears," said Mrs Dixon. "Now you've had a good talk together. It's so important to discuss the future, especially now that my darling Kaisu has to leave her beloved one for a long time. But she has promised to come back as soon as possible. I can hardly wait for the wedding now. My dear son, you are of course welcome when I'm here at home."

"Thank you, Mrs Dixon," said Andrew. "And thank you, too, for the wonderful party. Goodbye Mrs Dixon, and Miss E, and everyone, and goodbye darling."

Andrew planted a hurried kiss on my cheek, walked to the door that Frieda had opened for him, and with a smile and a nod he was gone.

163

Mrs Dixon put her hand on my shoulder, saying, "My dear Kaisu, I'm so pleased for thee. Your beloved one is a nice gentleman."

"Thank you, Mrs Dixon," I replied, "and thank you also for the lovely party."

I left to help the girls clear the table.

"What an ordeal she puts you through," said Klaudia. "I'd have refused to bring him here."

I told her that Andrew thought of it as a challenge to come and see her again, and to face the problem if there still was one.

"Luckily, thanks to everyone here being so discreet about their first encounter that terrible night, I think it's best forgotten now," I told her.

"Andrew is a hit with her now that he's her 'dear beloved son'," said Frieda.

"Thank goodness for that," I sighed.

I was very lucky, too, that our late-night party hadn't given me a complex or even too much worry. Poor Frieda would have lived with the shame of it for a long time, and Klaudia – who had never been allowed to go to such a party – didn't really know what she'd missed.

I'm sure it was for our spiritual well-being that Mrs Dixon suggested, one day, that she would take us to her church – the Friends' Meeting House – if we'd like to go.

"Thank you, we'd like it very much," we told her.

So Frieda and I joined Mrs Dixon in her Ford car. Klaudia, of course, didn't want to see that kind of thing.

We didn't have far to go to the beginning of the slum area towards the centre of town. Our destination was more like a red-brick house than a church. Inside, it looked like a simple and very bare meeting hall, with chairs in rows and, at one end, a wooden platform with a pulpit on it, where anybody could go and speak.

"This is the church my father built," Mrs Dixon told us. "He came here to pray and to preach, to save the poor people from destruction."

On the way home, she told us more.

"The chocolate drink-making was started to take men's minds off gin. There was so much suffering in those days and many needed the inner light to carry them through the life of hell. We all need inner light, thee and I, because there is no life without the light, and life is full of problems."

All the way home, she related her childhood memories of the church. Her life was so wrapped up in her memories that she could hardly let a day pass without unwrapping some of them for us.

They were all sweet and pleasant memories, because she wasn't one of those poor, undernourished slum children whose parents frequented the gin palaces. Her childhood had been spent in a luxurious house, near where she lived with us now, and we'd been shown many photographs of it.

Instead of being a plain Quaker home, it looked grand and opulent, and full of treasures.

In the large, high-ceilinged hall there were several palms among the paintings, carved and silk-covered sofas, inlaid tables and cabinets.

Chapter 22

The dark, pre-Christmas days had arrived. Some weeks before, Villis had started the central heating fire in the old Victorian boiler in the cellar, and it made all the difference in the main part of the house. We girls, however, relied on the gas fire for warmth.

The boiler room was full of coal, and Villis kept a little stool in front of the big stove. I sat on it one day, burning my old letters.

While I watched them catch light, I suddenly saw "Andrew Birminghamshire" written on one of them. I pulled it out quickly and read the letter again.

It was from a friend in Helsinki, and she wrote that she'd been faithfully buying an English newspaper in anticipation of the announcement of my engagement to "Andrew Birminghamshire"!

The letter had been written in the spring, months before I'd met Andrew, and I'd completely forgotten about it. Her intuition was better than my promise – that I wouldn't stay in England a day longer than a year.

With Christmas coming nearer, we were busy preparing the house, which we tried to clean better than ever before. On free afternoons, we walked to the village shops to buy cards and small presents for everyone in the house.

Andrew had made an arrangement with Mrs Dixon. He had asked if she would allow me to go to his parents' house on Christmas Day in the evening, and wanted me to stay the night there, too. He said he would bring me back on Boxing Day.

"Of course, my dear son. I'm so glad that Kaisu is at last going to meet your parents, now your mother is so much better," said Mrs Dixon. "I'm sure they're so much looking forward to meeting my darling Kaisu. Please give them my regards and best wishes."

I was certainly keen to meet his parents, although I was naturally apprehensive. As I was going to stay the night, I would have plenty of time to get to know them.

Mrs Dixon had asked Mrs Meyer to get a chicken for our Christmas lunch, and wanted her to tell us how to cook it. Mrs Meyer gave us an hilarious lecture on how to steam a Christmas pudding and how to stuff the chicken. We were confident that our Christmas lunch was going to be delicious.

We had each received small parcels from nearly all the people of the house, and we had put them in a laundry basket in our sitting room. We had decorated this room with Christmas roses and holly from the garden, as Mrs Meyer had told us was the English custom.

We had bought lots of candles, and we lit them on Christmas Eve after supper, and then turned off the lights. We settled down to listen to the radio, which had a lovely programme of carols sung in different countries in Europe.

We talked about our own Christmas customs and past festivities. We laughed at my story of Father Christmas and the bra, and how we would roll in the snow after a sauna. Then we opened our parcels.

There were no eggs to be counted that evening, because Villis had gone to spend Christmas with his friend, but Mrs Dixon came to see our festivities.

"I heard the music," she said, as she came in, "so I guessed you were enjoying a little party. I can see that you've also opened your parcels. I must go and fetch mine so you can have something sweet to eat."

She was soon back with her present – a large box of chocolate biscuits for us.

"And here is a little present for you," said Klaudia, handing Mrs Dixon our present of a cushion, which I had been sewing in great secrecy.

"I shall open my present tomorrow morning, as that is our custom," said Mrs Dixon. "We have never celebrated Christmas in a very elaborate way. It is, of course, the birthday of our Saviour, for whom we are thankful. Now, what kind of presents have you received?"

We eagerly showed her the books, sewing kits, stationery, scarves and socks, and she was interested to see who had given which presents to which person.

I had seen her in the nursery, wrapping up her presents of tins of biscuits for the household staff and boxes of chocolates for friends. We had been keeping our fingers crossed that we would have chocolates too – a taste of the family business – but our luck didn't go that far.

When I got up, Christmas morning was dark and wet. Tea was ready for the girls when they came down, and Mrs Dixon's morning tray had a couple of Christmas roses that I had picked from the garden the day before. Both girls had been reading well after midnight, so I cooked welcome bacon and eggs for us all, including Mrs Dixon.

We cleared the breakfast things away and, remembering we had to make an early start on the Christmas pudding, set to work. We put water in the saucepan, then a steamer on top of it, with the pudding inside and the lid on. Soon it was happily bubbling away on the gas. Simple – it was done in a few minutes.

We then did our usual rounds of the house, making Mrs Dixon's bed, tidying up and dusting the study and nursery, and cleaning the bathroom. Lastly, we cleaned our own rooms.

When it was time for elevenses, we were all ready for a cup of coffee, along with one of our new biscuits. I set off for the kitchen to make it, but in the hall I noticed an unusual smell.

When I opened the kitchen door, I was horrified to be greeted by thick smoke. In the middle of the smoke I could see that something terrible had happened: the Christmas pudding was scattered all over the floor, the saucepan had melted on the gas stove, and the lid had blown across the room to land on the table. The other girls rushed in behind me.

"Mein Gott!" cried Klaudia. "I'm sure there's something wrong with that recipe. Is this really the way to cook a Christmas pudding?"

"I know what the problem is," said Frieda. "We never checked the water." "That's obvious," I said, "and the gas must have been too high. Well, that's the end of our pudding."

Turning off the gas, I burst out laughing. Suddenly the situation was really funny. We had to go and tell Mrs Dixon. Luckily, she had the right Christmas spirit and didn't mind at all. After all, it was more of a loss to us, as we still weren't going to taste a Christmas pudding.

The rest of the cooking was more successful. Chicken with bacon, sausages and stuffing, roast potatoes, and Brussels sprouts – they all looked delicious. Magically, Mrs Dixon had found a tin of peaches – with custard, they were a good substitute for Christmas pudding.

We laid the table as nicely as possible, with holly and Christmas roses. Miss M, the old secretary, had arrived to share lunch with us. We lit candles in the food warmer and put all the vegetable dishes on it.

The meal started, as usual, with a long grace. Mrs Dixon closed her eyes, and bowed her curly white head over her arthritic hands, crossed on the table.

This time, she included a prayer for Andrew and me. "And please God, help this child to be a true wife to our dear son Andrew, and help him to be a good husband to my Finnish daughter." I was glad for this prayer, because I needed all the help I could get, living in a foreign country, and among strange people and customs.

Then, with her shaky hands, Mrs Dixon cut the chicken and served it with the vegetables. "Please can I have only a very little, as I am probably going to have another meal tonight," I asked, hoping she would give my share to the girls.

At last we were going to have a taste of our own cooking. I winked at Frieda and Klaudia, as a sign that it all tasted very good.

Mrs Dixon's meals always lasted a long time. We had finished long before the old ladies, who were again talking about the morning's disaster, as well as some other little accidents that had happened in the house long before our arrival.

Andrew called for me before I had finished the washing up. "I must go in to wish Mrs Dixon a merry Christmas, while you're getting ready. Do you agree?" asked Andrew. "But I will be short and sweet, because I'd like to be back home before the Queen's speech."

"Good idea, " I said, "but she will probably keep you there all afternoon if you let her."

In a few minutes, I was ready, wearing my best dress and fur coat. I had my small overnight case in my hand, and on the top of it were little presents for Andrew and his parents. At last, he came out of the drawing room, we said our goodbyes and were on the road.

It was a dark, drizzly, windy day. The streets that were usually so noisy and full of traffic were now empty of life. It seemed as though we were the only people in the middle of town.

Suddenly, the car stopped. Andrew and I looked at each other. "We've run out of petrol," he said."

"Oh help – and on Christmas Day," I said. "Are all the garages closed today?"

"Oh hell," said Andrew. "I hope I can find one that's open. I know I shouldn't have used that word today, but the worst things happen at the most inconvenient time." "Like on the way to a May Ball!" I remembered.

"I know one petrol station not too far away. With a bit of luck, it might be open," said Andrew, buttoning up his coat. He got out of the car and started walking into the wind. The garage was open, and soon we had a tank full of petrol.

"You see, this is a civilised country," said Andrew, getting back into the car. "We have services for the idiots, too!"

We reached his home just as the Queen's speech was ending. His parents were watching it on their new television. They had heard Andrew's car and came to the door to greet us.

His mother was short and plump – a pear-shaped woman, with grey curly hair and a friendly smile. His father was wearing a dark suit – he was much taller than his wife, with a longish face and a large nose that made his intelligent and lively eyes look small.

They both hugged me and said how glad they were to see me at last. I hugged them back, and gave them Mrs Dixon's regards. I inquired about Andrew's mother's leg, and said: "It must be like a Christmas present to have it working properly again."

The tea tray was ready for us in the dining room, where a lively fire was burning in the grate. "It's just a small tea, because we're going to have Christmas dinner later," said Andrew's mother. "I've been resting all morning, so I'm all right now," she added, as she poured us delicious-tasting tea – so different from Mrs Dixon's brew.

Andrew's parents were naturally interested in my background, my country, and my reasons for coming to England. I was a complete foreigner to them, and they said they'd never met a Finn before.

"We are such rare birds," I said, thinking that it was rather nice to be a Finn. And it always provided a good conversation opener at parties – something different from the usual talk about the weather.

Andrew and his father continued to talk about Finland. His father was a regular library user, and had found lots of facts about my distant and frozen homeland. His knowledge and interest flattered me and I told him so.

Soon, the first nervousness vanished. I liked these quiet, ordinary people, partly I suppose because I sensed that they liked me.

"Time for a drink," said Andrew. "Let's have a little sherry. It would shock Mrs Dixon to know that we're sinning like this, but never mind. We'll drink a toast to her."

The table had been beautifully laid, with candles and holly. "I've opened a rather nice bottle of wine," Andrew said. "It's a rare thing in our family, but we're celebrating today."

The turkey, with all the trimmings, was delectable – and what was more, we also had a Christmas pudding! There was a lot of laughter when I told them about Mrs Dixon's pudding.

"But despite that, and being in that strange place, you do like being in England, don't you dear?" asked Andrew's mother.

"Yes, I do," I told her. "England is so much more beautiful than I'd been led to believe. One can make endless discoveries about all sorts of things. I have so much to learn and, even more, to appreciate."

"It will take a lifetime to discover London, let alone the rest of the country," said Andrew's father.

After the meal, I insisted on helping with the washing up, which Andrew's father did. "I'm quite good at it now," he said.

"I've had lots of training while Mother has been poorly." "He doesn't like leaving it to the cleaning lady," remarked Andrew's mother, as she brought in the coffee.

We opened our presents, which were all books. There was a book about the history of England for me; a picture book of Finland for Andrew's parents; and another small one, plus a box of cigars, for Andrew.

It was late when we went upstairs. My room was opposite the parents' room, and the moonlight was streaming in through the large window.

The real coffee had done its trick – I didn't feel at all sleepy. In the dark, my thoughts went back over the day, and Andrew's family who had accepted and adopted me, as I had them. It hadn't been as difficult as I'd imagined.

Suddenly, I heard the door opening, and Andrew was standing there in the moonlight, in his dressing gown. "Thank goodness it's you and not a ghost," I whispered. "Can't you sleep either?"

Sitting on the side of my bed, he said: "We must be very quiet or Mother will hear us." I pulled him down and kissed him.

"Have you had a good Christmas?" he asked. "I've had a super Christmas, my darling, and so much better than Mrs Dixon's," I told him, holding him tight.

He pulled back, and in the moonlight I saw that he was on his guard – and also that he was frightened of me. He stood up and said: "I must go now. Good night, and sleep well." He stepped quietly out of the room.

Astonished as I was, I could only admire him. What a gentleman he was – cool to the end. Does he really love me? If so, why doesn't he say it? Why did he come in if he was afraid of what his mother might say, at his age?

He was certainly very reserved, but then perhaps all people were the same – still hanging onto the old values and traditions of the Victorian era. Even the young people, who'd had to grow up quickly during the war and change their whole lives and behaviour, were determined still to cherish the old ways of life and customs.

In Finland, we'd also had to become adults too quickly. Our frugal life during the war – both while we were fighting and for years afterwards as we worked to pay off our war debts to Russia – had at last become pleasant again, leaving us more free and relaxed to expand in spirit and wealth, and to explore the world.

My thoughts were muddled. What was right and what was wrong in these circumstances? And who was I to pass judgment on English behaviour?

All English people were blindly respected in Finland. All women were ladies and all men were gentlemen. They could do nothing wrong, or if they did, they said smilingly: "So sorry. I beg your pardon." Who could ever be angry with such politeness?

Satisfied with this, I slept at last, long into the next day.

Chapter 23

A delicious smell of bacon and eggs woke me up. After a leisurely breakfast and a second cup of coffee, Andrew promised to drive me back to Tennessee.

His mother's farewell to me was: "I always wanted another daughter, and now I've got one."

Back at Tennessee, the girls were naturally interested to hear what Andrew's parents were like.

"Oh, very sweet," I told them. "They're old and not physically agile, but they're pleasant and relaxed people. I could feel at home there."

I gave them a lengthy report of my visit.

"They adore Andrew," I told them. "His word is their law, and he is their god as well as being their son.

"Both daughters are more than 10 years older than Andrew. The elder one – she is the more loved and loving one – was a beautiful lady. Unfortunately, she died some years ago, leaving a little boy and a husband, who has since remarried.

"The younger sister is a real blue-stocking. At the ripe age of 40, she has recently married a Cambridge academic, and is now expecting a baby."

I had to describe the night's menu and show the girls my presents.

"I suppose you have no appetite for this sort of food, after such a gorgeous dinner last night?" asked Klaudia, dishing out the sausages for our lunch.

"Of course I have," I told her, "and I will eat one, to show you."

Boxing Day brought beautiful weather – the wind had dropped and the sun had appeared.

"Let's go for a walk in the park, for a change," I suggested.

"I can't. I'm too exhausted," said Klaudia.

"Exhausted by what?" I asked, laughing.

"By living," she said, curling herself into an armchair with a book.

"Poor Klaudia," I said, pulling on my gloves. "You haven't started to live yet. Your turn will come. You just wait – someone will come and snatch you up and make you a mother of his children."

"We poor women – is that really all we want from life?" said Frieda, shaking her head.

"Who can we blame for that," I asked. "The instinct to reproduce is too strong. But you can get the benefit of being in love, and being loved, and the happiness and achievement that go with it," I said, adding, "I hope."

But Frieda was in the mood to argue.

"So you think that if we haven't experienced those things, we haven't lived?" she said.

"Not fully, I suppose," I replied.

"We can go on forever talking about life," said Frieda, "but shall we go for a walk first, while the sun is still out?"

She opened the door to the sunny outside world.

We walked down the road to the wild part of the park. I had escaped here sometimes, and had sat by the little stream, watching its secret life busying around it.

That life was instinctive. We people were the only ones who could decide about our lives – or, at least, attempt to decide. We were ambitious, and we wanted a life just one step better than was fitting for our social class. That was our secret desire and hope, but our lack of capability often stopped that social climb, although it didn't always stop the desire. We complained about our physical disabilities, but seldom complained about our brain power.

"I am happy too," said Frieda. "I shall have a very good job in Ulm, with possibilities of promotion, when I go back there. It's already waiting for me but I'll have a little holiday with my family first. I've missed them, but not as much as Klaudia has missed her mother."

"You girls are lucky," I told her. "You have someone to miss, and someone to miss you."

There were crowds of people in the park, all in their Sunday best. Little boys were trying out their new bicycles, and little girls were pampering their new dolls, behaving like small mothers.

There were older people walking with younger ones, some holding onto younger arms. It was the season of good will and family togetherness, and they had the time to enjoy it. Perhaps tomorrow the older ones would be back on their own, in their quiet and lonely homes.

We were absorbed in looking at people and trying to guess what they did for a living. Hearing their accent, we could decide whether they were professional or trades people.

"Have you noticed," asked Frieda, "how much easier it is to tell where a man comes from, or what he does, than it is a woman?"

"I think women are more adaptable than men, and perhaps more ambitious," I said. "They like to show off their husband's wealth or profession, as much as the husbands like to glory in it."

We walked quietly for a while, and then Frieda said, "I fear your future life here will be quite difficult. You'll have to get used to a different social life than we have at Tennessee, and to be a hostess for your professional husband, especially if he goes into politics."

"Thank goodness I'm a foreigner," I said. "I hope it will be easier to learn if I don't already know the wrong way. Let's go home for tea. I know the correct way to serve that now!"

I put my arm through Frieda's.

For us, the New Year came in as quietly as the old one had gone out, in our sitting room, listening to Auld Lang Syne on the radio.

Andrew had told me there was not going to be any party for him, either. There was no time for it, he had said.

Mrs Meyer had alerted us to the fact that the January sales were starting. It was a good opportunity to buy presents – I had more room for them in my luggage now, as I'd used Andrew's home to store all the clothes I didn't want in Finland.

At last, I was ready to leave Tennessee. It had been my home for a whole year, and I'd grown very fond of it, and of my "English mother".

I had come here for a quiet year of study, and it had become a most exciting year – a year that had changed my life even more than the war had.

On a cold January morning, Andrew came to drive me to the station. I had kissed everybody goodbye, and I could still feel Mrs Dixon's soft, downy cheek against my own when we drove out of the gate, waving and shouting, "I'll be back!"

One year, and not a day longer, had been my promise. Now I had to swallow my words. I was coming back, but not to this house.

Those wet streets, those little front gardens where various evergreens were glistening in the morning sun, still damp with yesterday's rain – I shall see you all again, I thought.

"Did you make a list of all the things you have to do in Finland?" Andrew asked.

"Yes, I did," I assured him.

"I'm really sorry to send you there alone, " he said, "but I believe that it's better that I'm not there to influence you too much about your decisions when it comes to disposing of your home. In a way, clearing your home will be sad, but luckily your friends will become our friends now. Do ask them to come and see us as soon as our home is ready."

"Yes, I will," I said.

He went on: "I'd so much like to come with you, but firstly I'm terribly busy, and secondly I couldn't help you very much. My Finnish is non-existent. You must teach me some useful words."

"I will," I said, realising that he didn't even know "I love you" in Finnish.

I had a sudden idea. I would buy a silver gilt cigarette box for him as a wedding present, and have it engraved inside the lid. My love message would be there forever, for him to see.

We arrived at the station, and Andrew called a porter to carry my case. I was clinging to his arm, suddenly feeling very lonely and sorry for myself. A few tears were rolling down my cheeks as I whispered my promise to love him forever.

I climbed into my carriage. Andrew jumped up after me, kissed me, and said, "No tears now, or emotions. Be a brave girl and come back to me as soon as possible. Look after yourself, and write to me. Write soon, and often."

I promised everything. He stepped out of the carriage, the train started to roll forward, and his serious face faded into the mist.

My journey to Finland was not easy. We had to cross three different seas. It was cold, and the fields were frozen. There was only a little snow until we reached the middle of Sweden. From then on, we had the protective cover of snow over everything, against the hard frost.

The journey went without too much trouble, and even allowed me a short time to shop in Stockholm. Then I was on the boat again, eating dinner, enjoying a good night's sleep, before we arrived in Turku.

I had a day in the city, seeing friends, and then went on to Helsinki, where some old friends were meeting me at the station. I had known them since my teens, and they took loving care of me.

179

The sauna had been heated up for the evening, to welcome me home. The dry heat penetrated to my bones, and even made me feel lighter in my heart. We sat over dinner for a long time that night, talking and planning my long stay.

One of the first things to do was to go to my old office. I had written to them, resigning my job, so they knew about my engagement. They wanted to see my ring, and it was certainly worth showing off. It was unusual to have a diamond engagement ring – in Finland, we have only a plain gold ring, with another added to it at the wedding ceremony.

"It's so gorgeous that I wouldn't mind going to any foggy, smoggy, dirty country just to have it," said one friend. She had been only to Hull, in a boat!

"Well, I'm going back because I'm in love," I told her.

My friends made such a lovely song and dance about my engagement – literally. There was a party for me, where I was presented with silver cutlery. Only the best was good enough to take back to England!

I caught a bad cold, which turned to flu, but with good care I was up and about again in a few days.

I wanted to go to church to hear my banns being read. Was it the flu or emotion that made my eyes moist when I heard our names being read out?

I was busy in town. I had to sell my insurance and my flat, dispose of my furniture and household goods, my skis and my bicycle. I had to shop for something new, and Finnish, for my new home. And there were several trunk-loads of clothes and other things to be sent on ahead to England.

I went to the country to see my aunt and uncle. They were like parents to me and, naturally, were very anxious that I had made the right decision.

It was still quite unusual to have enough money, courage and opportunity to travel abroad, and even more so to marry in a foreign country.

In the year since I'd last been in Finland, I'd noticed a difference. The country was better off, with more food and more goods in the shops. We were still poor, but now we were optimistic. We certainly weren't finished, as Stalin had predicted.

Now we had only to come out of our shells, see the rest of the world, and learn from that experience.

Back in Helsinki, I wanted to give a farewell party for all my friends. Every one of them wanted to come and see how happy I was going to be, as I left them forever to vanish into a strange world.

At first, I was slightly self-conscious about telling them too much, but I noticed no jealousy about my luck in marrying abroad, so I was happy to radiate happiness and excitement.

At the end of my time in Finland, I had to leave for the station. Friends came with me – laughing, crying, waving, hugging and kissing, just as though I was going to the end of the world. It was sweet sorrow to leave.

Everybody at the station was looking at this happy crowd.

"All of you must come to see me in England," I told them, "but not all together! But do come, and we'll have another party there."

I climbed into the carriage, opened the window and waved my handkerchief until I could no longer see their faces in the wonderful luminous twilight of that cold February afternoon.

The train gathered speed and the freezing air made my nose more red than my tears had done. I closed the window, sat down, still with my coat on, and stared at the empty seat in front of me.

So this was it. The beginning of my new life. The old one I knew so well was left behind, and now it was Andrew's life that I was going to live. And all because I loved him, wanted him, and wasn't frightened of the future.

I took Andrew's letters out and read them again. They were sweet, loving letters, anxious about my well-being and home-coming.

Chapter 24

Although the journey was long, it wasn't too monotonous. Again, there was the overnight ferry, with a long sleep in my cabin. Then there was the train, and two more ferries, and I was back in foggy London town.

Everything looked cold and damp. Anxiously, I hoped Andrew would not be late, because the train was on time. And he was not.

I saw him standing on the platform, hands deep in overcoat pockets, a porter with a trolley standing beside him. Andrew looked very distinguished in his dark city suit and coat.

He saw me, waved and came towards me.

"Welcome home. Are you all right? I'm so glad you're back safely," he greeted me.

I had already learned not to show too much emotion, but he must have seen from my eyes, which I couldn't take away from him, that I was glad to be with him again. I was safe and secure with his arms around me.

"I'm so glad to be back," I said. "I have so much to tell you but I must see to the luggage first."

I kissed him on the cheek.

Some of my luggage had not arrived – Andrew quickly found a railway official, and I saw Andrew tipping him and giving our address so the missing items could be sent on to me. The rest was loaded into the car.

"Ready?" asked Andrew. "Mother is waiting for us for lunch. We should just make it."

We easily drove through London, which was so much busier than Helsinki. So it should be, I reminded myself – London has twice the population of the whole of Finland. It is ten times as big as Helsinki.

It always surprised me that anyone could find their way around in London. Could I ever get to know it that well?

When we drove through the city, it held a wonderful promise of enjoyment for me. There was the theatre I attended with the captain, more than a year ago. There were the shops I'd seen before, and there were exciting-looking streets that I wanted to explore.

"It's so damp and cold, with no sun. It was like this when I left, and I suppose it's comforting that it's much the same today. London doesn't seem to change much," I said to Andrew.

"I too remember that depressing day when you left," Andrew said, "but I hope we'll have more sunshine today to welcome you home. I can see the blue of a sailor's collar, which means the clouds will go away. I'm so glad you're safely back here."

Once we were on the open road, he started to tell me his news. The big excitement was that he had bought a house. A client had, for some reason, refused to take a house that was being built for him. Andrew saw his chance and took it.

"It was a lucky strike," he said. "It's in Solihull, not far from town – only half an hour – and still on the edge of the country."

"How lovely," I said, excitedly. "I'm dying to see it."

I asked, cautiously, if it had central heating.

"Central heating?" Andrew said in astonishment. "Of course not. We're in England. We don't need central heating here. It's never cold enough."

"Well, we'll have lovely coal fires like your parents have," I said. "They're so cosy."

I didn't protest, because I knew the decision had already been made.

"The wedding will be in three weeks' time, in our local church," Andrew told me. "You'll see it tomorrow. It's small and old, but very nice. We must go to see the vicar as well.

"The reception will be at an old manor, outside town and in a lovely park. And we must send the invitations out tomorrow, too.

"I've arranged for you to stay in my brother-in-law's house until the wedding," he continued. "I don't like you to go to Mrs Dixon's house more than once again. You're too familiar with them there."

"Yes, I must go there once to collect the few things I've left with the girls," I said. "I'll invite them all to the church – do you agree?"

"As you wish," Andrew said. "But now you're marrying me, you'll be on a different social standing with the servants in that house who have naturally called you by your Christian name. So it's better that you don't meet them any more."

"I understand," I said, without conviction.

We had left the sight of green hills and herds of cows, which were even in winter happily grazing on the grass, and drove through the Birmingham suburbs to Andrew's home.

His parents came to the door to greet us, and were just as excited as I was. We were soon sitting, relaxed and laughing, at the lunch table.

Andrew left for the office, giving me the chance to get to know his parents better. That evening, after supper, Andrew drove me to his brother-in-law's house.

Malcolm was an accountant – jolly, stocky, easy-going, and with a red face and laughing eyes. His second wife, Elizabeth, was a small, slim woman with lots of black curly hair and the same rosy complexion as her husband's.

They both welcomed me in a very friendly way, almost over-doing it in their efforts to make me feel at home. After I'd been taken to my large room, along with my cases, we sat by the fire, talking, planning and joking.

"We're glad you haven't forgotten your English," said Malcolm. "From now on, it can only get better. You're going to make me feel my age when I escort you to the altar."

"I hope not," I said, "but I'm grateful to you because I'd otherwise have to have Mrs Dixon and then I'd never reach the altar without some disaster on the way."

The three weeks went by quickly, as we organised the church, the music, the flowers, the dress . . . . I missed my darling mother when I chose the wedding dress, because she had had such good taste in clothes. I especially missed her as I wanted her to share in my happiness.

Canon Barrett, who was to marry us, offered to give me communion any time I wanted it, even though I was not a member of the Anglican church.

A large and wonderful collection of wedding presents arrived at the house, among them a dozen white linen face towels from Mrs Dixon – all of them old, but beautifully mended by hand!

A long time before, Andrew had accepted an invitation for us to attend a party on the night before our wedding. What a surprise it was to the other guests when they heard that we were going to be married the next day. It was obviously not a proper thing to do. All the same, the other guests drank a toast to our happiness. Soon afterwards, we left.

I was not nervous about the next day, and slept very well – my last night as a single girl.

A knock on the door woke me up on my wedding day. Elizabeth was there with a breakfast tray.

"You need lots of time to dress, and to rest before you have to leave," she said.

"Thank you so much," I said, with a tear in my eye. "You and Malcolm have looked after me so well. I would have been lost without you, and I'm so grateful to you both."

"It's been a very interesting time for us, too," said Elizabeth. "If you need any help dressing, just call me."

I did not call her. I dressed by myself, feeling lonely in the silence of the bedroom.

The flowers arrived in good time, and I was ready to leave for the church. The day had started with a mist, but soon the wind was blowing and the sun came out. It was a typical spring day – cold wind but a warm sun by midday.

For me, the day was like a dream. Yet it was all true. I was so proud to be marrying in England, and even more proud to be marrying a man whom I loved so much.

I realised that I didn't know Andrew well, but somehow that did not matter. He was an Englishman – very English – and as a lawyer hoping to get into politics, a very trustworthy man.

He had an air of quiet confidence that I found very attractive. Importantly, he provided me with the safety and security I craved, and I felt cared for and protected for the first time in my life.

Looking back, I can see that he needed to marry to enable him to enter the world of politics; I was young and pretty, but shy and unworldly, and I had no close family or friends, so he could mould me as he pleased.

On my wedding day, though, I was so proud to think that I was going to become part of his life. Having lost my Finnish home and my family during the Second World War, I was no longer frightened of the future. And such losses in my early life had made me realise how important and precious home was for a stable life.

So the thought of my own permanent home gave me immense joy and new hope. It meant a new challenge to make life better, limited only by my imagination.

It was with such lovely, hopeful thoughts that my mind was filled as I made my way to the church.

As I walked down the aisle, I felt everyone's eyes on me, but I saw only the beautiful flowers in front of me. The choir were dressed in their red tunics, with white collars, and Andrew was standing in front of the altar, straight and stiff, near Canon Barrett in his white and gold surplice.

The music filled the old stone church, inspiring me with the importance of the occasion. It was as though I was acting the part of a bride before I suddenly realised it was for real – it was my life, my day, and my husband-to-be waiting for me.

I remembered to promise to love, honour and cherish, and to obey him until death do us part, and he promised to love me and with his body to worship me, with his worldly goods endow me, and we promised to keep each other in sickness and in health. It was truly the most demanding commitment one can ever make.

The wedding breakfast was a lunch in the dining room of the old manor house. We greeted our relatives and friends, and I was grateful that they had played an important part in making my day so memorable.

After lunch and the toasts, we gathered in the garden for farewells, before leaving for the honeymoon.

The park around the manor house looked bright in the sunshine, and the old larches and pines stood grand and sombre above the yellow carpet of daffodils.

I found Andrew on his own, standing at the edge of the lawn, looking at this beautiful sight.

I walked up to him and squeezed his hand, but he did not respond. I turned to him, adoringly, and said: "We're married now. We're man and wife, and I'm so happy."

Andrew turned to me. His eyes froze me. His face stiffened and became absolutely white. He said nothing – he just stared at me in horror, as though he'd seen an awful ghost.

I looked at his frightened, distant and cold eyes for a long time. I too was frightened now, and a chill swept through me.

"My God, he's made a mistake, after all this," I thought. I felt stunned, helpless and sad. I couldn't think straight.

Through the tears that I felt forming, I forced a smile. I took his limp arm and squeezed it against me.

"Let's go. They're waiting for us," I said quietly.

I was desperate. Why this? His cold stare followed me like thunder from the sky. I saw now that my husband Andrew had changed – and changed completely.

He had made a terrible mistake. He had miscalculated and I was only a ghost to him.

In front of that lovely old grey manor house, our guests were now feeling jolly after a good lunch. Luckily, everything happened quickly, like heavenly clouds rushing into a stormy sky.

After quick hugs and kisses, smiling and waving happily, they watched us drive out through the manor's grand gates, off to our honeymoon in Eastbourne, unaware of the silent storm inside us.

Kaisu's whole life was ahead of her when this picture, left, was taken in Finland, before she came to England as an au pair at the age of 28.

Tennessee was a big house in Moor Green Lane, Moseley, Birmingham. Mrs Helen Dixon – a member of the Cadbury family – lived there on her own, with a huge retinue of helpers. This picture above shows the back of the house, overlooking the delightful four-acre gardens.

Mrs Helen Dixon saw her au pair girls as her children. She is pictured, second left, holding Tigger the cat. Far left is Frieda; second from right is Klaudia; Kaisu is far right.

190

Once a year, Mrs Dixon treated her staff, past and present, to a Bank Holiday outing. The destination was a house called Wynds Point, in Malvern, which was the holiday home of the Cadbury family and had previously been owned by Jenny Lynd, the opera singer. Everyone travelled in this hired bus.

Once married, Kaisu played an important part in her ambitious husband's political life. Her working wardrobe was a selection of glamorous dresses, as she attended a wide range of public events, giving speeches and featuring in the local newspapers.

Kaisu's dearest wish was to have a child. Despite his pre-marriage promises of a large number of children, Kaisu's husband Andrew was repelled by any demonstration of physical affection. To silence her pleas for a child, he presented her with a poodle, which she named Bonnie.

This picture was taken at the time of Kaisu's divorce, when she was living in Highgate, London. She worked first for the BBC World Service's Finnish section, and then as librarian at Hornsey College of Art.

Kaisu lived in Spain for many years, later remarrying and returning to England. Now widowed, she lives near Cambridge.

Part Two

Chapter 25

The shock of Andrew's sudden change in attitude towards me hit hard. I felt as if my world had suddenly come to an end.

We drove silently for a long time. I secretly tried to look at Andrew's face; it was serious, but not white any more. With a heavy heart, I expected him to say something about what had happened in the garden, but he never did.

It should have been discussed, but it never was. I was afraid to ask about it, and Andrew had no courage to say anything about it either. I had to try to forget it, which of course I could not.

I was sure he had made a mistake by asking me to be his wife. In time, I would have to find out for myself whether I was right. Meanwhile, I tried to think if I had done or said something terrible to hurt him and send him into this icy silence.

I decided to talk to him, to try to gauge his mood.

"It's been a lovely day. Have you enjoyed it?" I asked him.

There was a long silence, before he said "Yes", but he didn't sound convinced.

"Everybody seemed to enjoy the lunch," I said, and then I tried to turn our thoughts to our honeymoon.

"When do you think we'll be there?" I asked.

"For dinner, I hope," was his reply. Then he added, "I hope you aren't going to show off about the fact that we're on our honeymoon."

After that, he was silent.

We arrived at the hotel in time for dinner, and ate there every evening that week. The hotel was not the grandest in Eastbourne, but it was the second best. We fitted in well and I didn't show off joyful newly-wed emotions to other guests – not that there was much to show off.

I tried to act as if I had been married all my life. Quietly, I smiled and said to myself, "I have been married one day, two days, three days and three hours. So this is what it is all about."

Of course, it should not have been what it was all about, but that is more or less how it was.

The big event of a honeymoon – the love-making and consummation of the marriage – didn't happen at all. There wasn't even a slight pretence of it, and there wouldn't be for another six months.

I blamed the fact that I had my period. Thank goodness I did have something to blame, otherwise I would have been desperate and very suspicious of life's intentions. I was so eager to be romantic, in my new sheer nightie, but the result was a polite rejection. He always quickly found something to do or say, that easily stopped my foolish thoughts.

Happy honeymoon togetherness was not apparent, and the relationship remained cool and formal.

Somewhere, Andrew had found an old book, called "Brush up your English". He took this with us on our walks, and I was expected to read it on the beach. Sometimes he even left me alone with the book, giving me a chapter to read and testing me when he returned an hour or two later.

Why I didn't rebel against this treatment, I don't know. Neither did I know where he spent the time away from me. I was afraid to ask because I guessed his answer would not be the truth. Perhaps he had to telephone his office – this was always on his mind and a talking point between us. Perhaps he had a friend nearby.

I started to feel very distant from him. I felt like a stranger in town – even in the whole country – without any friends. Sometimes I felt like a teenage girl learning about life and busily observing his odd behaviour. I felt I was often treated like one, too.

195

In the evenings, we talked like strangers about general and ordinary things, but never about anything intimate or emotional. I would have liked to ask him what he thought about married life, but that would have been out of order and created a long silence.

It was impossible for me to feel like, or act as, a newly-married woman. Was this really going to be life's pattern for ever, or could I change it? If so, how? What should I do?

Sometimes, I felt slightly desperate, but I sensibly pushed such thoughts away. I told myself life would be easier if I didn't care or worry too much and tried to take everything easy. Let life be a surprise and see later how it would mould itself, I decided.

It helped that I wasn't familiar with married life. I had nearly forgotten my previous home life in Finland, so cruelly torn apart by the war. Even recently, when visiting other couples' houses, I had seen only glimpses of their Sunday best behaviour.

Nor did I have a mother to tell me about the problems and joys of married life. In fact, I didn't have anyone to tell me anything. So I had to form my own ideas of married life.

Andrew obviously did not want to be married. And he wanted to keep me in ignorance of my rights, and quash my ideas of them before they took hold.

I had no bosom friends with whom to discuss life's problems, and in any case I would have been too afraid and too proud to reveal my unhappy state to anybody. I knew it wasn't the English way to talk about or show your emotions.

On our way home from Eastbourne, Andrew decided to visit an old Cambridge friend, who had sent us a beautiful silver sugar bowl as a wedding present.

He had married early, and he and his Swedish wife already had two children. I was really looking forward to meeting Greta. I was sure she'd be like a long-lost cousin and a kindred spirit.

We arrived for a Scandinavian lunch at their home, which was full of toys and signs of toddlers' activities. Andrew introduced us. Shaking hands with Greta, I happily greeted her with "Hello".

On our way home, Andrew told me that was wrong. I should have said, as I usually did, "How do you do?" Greta should not have been an exception. I remembered my lesson ever after.

We settled in Andrew's parents' home in Birmingham for the first few months of our marriage, because our new home was still unfinished. Theirs was a double-fronted old vicarage, where half the downstairs had been made into one of Andrew's offices, to which a secretary came every day.

We had Andrew's large bedroom, and slept innocently in his double bed, like brother and sister. We shared the only bathroom in the house. It was plain, large and always cold, except at bath times when it was bursting with hot steam.

My in-laws were very welcoming, helpful and kind to me, and I never had a bad word or thought about them. My mother-in-law was very kind and helpful in a material way, but she would never ask or talk about the private world of anyone's marriage. Life was still ruled by hypocritical Victorian views of morality and convention.

How I missed my own mother. She would have seen my life through my eyes and comforted me. My mother-in-law would probably have seen it too, but could not have said anything to comfort me.

Such unhappy thoughts followed me all my married life, distorting my deep love for Andrew.

I remembered my mother's last letter to me, sent as I sought refuge at my uncle's house in the Finnish countryside when war was declared.

My uncle was away fighting, but my grandmother and my aunt, whom I had never met before, were at home.

Surprisingly quickly, I received a letter from my mother, asking me to stay there away from the bombings and to be humble to my grandmother and aunt. Now I was humble to my in-laws as well. I was not there to criticise their English way of living.

My father-in-law was a quiet, retired, intelligent man, who had worked for Birmingham City Council in the transport department. He was a great reader and always helpful to his wife. They had a very settled and organised life, so there was never much talk or discussion in the house. I knew that my arrival disturbed their life, but it was going to be for only a few months.

My mother-in-law busied herself by frequently taking me to town to choose curtain materials, carpets and even fireplaces for our new home, while my father-in-law was left to organise tea for our return.

Eventually, Andrew took some time off and we went to all the furniture stores in London.

Of course, I had a fixed idea about our home, with nothing but modern Scandinavian furniture allowed, but as there seemed to be none in the whole of England, we settled for traditional English furniture and antiques.

One of the first things we did after the honeymoon was to invite all Andrew's friends, who had kindly given us such wonderful presents, for a dinner dance at the manor where we'd held our wedding reception. The occasion was a chance for me to buy my first long evening dress from Bond Street. I would eventually acquire quite a collection.

We had the manor to ourselves and enjoyed the evening enormously. As Andrew didn't want me to sit next to him at dinner, it was a good opportunity for me to get to know his friends better.

Spring turned into summer, and I was busy and happy getting our new home ready. It was a new, detached house in a crescent on the outskirts of Birmingham. The lawn had already been laid and some trees and roses planted, although Andrew had been too busy to take much notice of it.

In the early summer, we finally moved in. Now we had a chance to settle into married life at last.

Our home had four bedrooms. I planned to use one small one as a nursery; one was Andrew's study; the third was a guest room and the largest was our bedroom, with the two single beds Andrew had insisted on.

I'd left the little nursery unfinished, and had previously tried to talk to Andrew about starting a family. He just said we would think about it when we'd moved in.

How silly we were to have had only one bathroom, no fitted wardrobes, and no central heating. Andrew had told me those things didn't belong in an English home.

Our breakfast room, where we had meals when we were alone, had a fireplace with a constant fire burning in it. However, I didn't have much time to sit in front of it as Andrew had joined the Conservative Party and was kept very busy.

Already, he had fought a council election, and lost. He was happy about this, saying he did not want to be what he called "a dustbin politician". He had his sights set on something far higher – he wanted a real Parliamentary election fight.

That opportunity was soon offered to him, and we started a three-year battle to win a seat for him in the House of Commons.

Chapter 26

As soon as our home was presentable, we invited Mrs Dixon for tea. Mr Knight, her chauffeur, brought her to our house in her old black taxi-like Ford.

Andrew had taken the afternoon off work, and had all the time in the world to talk to her about the Bible.

I served tea in my well-practised way, and had made sure in advance that all the ashtrays, cigarettes and bottles had been taken to the next-door neighbour's. This was just as well, as she inspected every room in the house.

Even then something dreadful happened. In the middle of Mrs Dixon's explanation of the origins of Jews and Arabs, I noticed that a cigarette had fallen between two sofa cushions in front of her. Saying a quick prayer, I plucked it away like a hawk, hoping she had not seen it.

Andrew was a member of the Birmingham Law Society Committee. It was decided that this committee, with their wives, were to make a day trip to the House of Commons.

We started early in the morning, travelling by coach to Richmond, where we had lunch.

The "bar" on the coach had been opened indecently early, and jolly sounds of "Splice the mainbrace" were often heard, and again later on the boat that had been booked to take us all the way to Westminster Pier.

There, we were met by Selwyn Lloyd (then MP for Wirral, but later Foreign Secretary and Chancellor of the Exchequer) and Edith Pitt (MP for Birmingham Edgbaston).

We saw the Speaker's procession, and from the gallery we experienced one of the most sensational days in the House of Commons – the Critchell Down debate by Winston Churchill and Herbert Morrison.

Morrison fiercely attacked, with Churchill cleverly but with great physical difficulty rising time after time to respond.

In the middle of this fighting speech, our tea on the river terrace was announced, but Andrew wanted to stay to the surprise end of the speech.

The House was very tense, until the final uproar at the unbelievable result – the resignation of the government minister responsible, Sir Thomas Dugdale.

The day had been memorable, and a fine dinner at a hotel in Woodstock crowned it all.

Before our own political fight started, we were keen to visit Finland and Scandinavia. It was wonderful to think that Andrew wanted to see my country.

We sailed from London in an old Finnish ship which, before the war, had already been on the London-Helsinki route. But we had had to give it to the Russians as payment towards our war debts.

Now the ship was quite shabby, but the cabins were big and it was comfortable enough, especially as there weren't many passengers. Some of them were going to the ship's new home port of Leningrad.

Our meals were very memorable, depending on the chef's mood, and very Russian. We had a bowl of caviar on our breakfast table each morning. As our table companions – two young English and French couples – didn't like it, we had a feast each day. I loved caviar and taught Andrew to like it too.

The week on board was a welcome rest for Andrew. He had been very busy in his office, his different associations and his political pursuits; after our holiday, he was also going to be chairman of the Round Table.

With all this work on his mind, I tried to remind him again about having a child. It was a wasted hope.

He answered, seriously, that we would think about it next winter.

"But I would love to have a baby. It's one of the reasons I married you," I told him.

There was only a long silence as an answer.

Asking for physical love would have been rude or even obscene, and wouldn't have helped the situation. I just had to wait. Even a romantic sea cruise like this couldn't get Andrew in the mood for love. I was becoming sad and quiet, and could hardly stop thinking about it.

We docked at Helsinki on a lovely summer's day, and spent similar days in town and country with my relations and friends. How lovely it was to meet them again, and I was so proud to show Andrew around.

Although my friends couldn't easily understand the different language, they must have noticed how kind and gentlemanly he was.

We took a boat to Stockholm, where we stayed for a few days, and then went on to Oslo and Copenhagen. I had been to all these cities and was eager to show them to Andrew and to some Americans who were staying in the same hotels as us.

It was a lovely but loveless holiday, as were all other holidays to come in our ten-year-long marriage.

Back at home, I had to start learning to drive. After six lessons, my teacher crashed his car so Andrew taught me a few times. I didn't learn much driving but I did learn a few swear words.

Back at the driving school, and with a patient teacher, I confidently passed my test at the second try. After that, I would sometimes drive Andrew's parents to Cambridge to see their daughter Carol and new grandson Mark.

I was also getting more involved in politics, to help Andrew. We went to various conferences, and met and got to know some members of Parliament, including the Prime Minister Harold Macmillan and his wife, Lady Dorothy, who were always enthusiastically telling me about their visits and experiences in Finland, and what a wonderful feeling of freedom there was after Russia.

I went on a public speaking course, as I now had to make speeches when opening bazaars, starting rallies, and giving a vote of thanks after meetings.

At first I was terrified, but then I remembered the advice given to me by Mrs Anne Chamberlain, widow of the late Prime Minister Neville Chamberlain. We had been sitting together and I had to get up to speak. She noticed my fear and said calmly, "Just get up, take a deep breath, let your eyes wander over people, and you will see how their eyes follow yours because they are keen to hear what you have to say; then just start speaking."

This advice helped me a lot.

I was a vice-president of the local Conservative Women's Association, and I sat on the platform looking young and pretty. I think that people forgave me a lot because I was an oddity – a foreigner.

That was my special worry, too, though. While I had lost my Finnish nationality and gained a British one, I had not lost my foreign accent. However, Birmingham people never seemed to mind it – on the contrary, in fact, I felt I was loved by them. They were certainly curious about me, as there were often pictures of me in the papers, taken at the various evening functions we now had to attend. There was even a long interview with me, with a large picture, in the local paper.

There were ladies' night dances for all Andrew's associations, as well as his friends' ones. I often felt that my evening dress was my working dress. After all, Birmingham loved its evening life. But although it was the second city, it lacked the sophistication of London.

Even if my life was loveless, it was interesting and so often provided a new experience and challenge. And life was not only in Birmingham – it expanded to the weekend and annual conferences in London and beyond.

Quite often, at social functions, when Andrew had vanished to the bar with other gentlemen, someone would come up to me with a worried look, but trying to joke, and say, "I hear that you're Finnish. Isn't that a communist country? I wouldn't be surprised if you were a Russian spy."

"Of course I'm a Russian spy," I would joke; but only in the early years, before I realised that many people knew very little about Finland and were seriously worried about the safety of their country. After all, the spy Kim Philby and company were still alive.

I was rather touched by this attitude and it seemed quite understandable, as the Cold War was raging and Russia was not seen as a trustworthy friend. I had also become very Anglicised, and defended England as much as I had always defended Finland against unfair criticism.

I had to learn quickly to remember all about people I met and on whose vote Andrew was dependent. I had to remember whose children were in New Zealand, whose in Australia or Canada, and what they did.

Andrew had no time or willingness to help me, and there was no-one else to rely on. I often felt helpless and lonely, especially as Andrew was out nearly every evening of the week, apparently at meetings.

Sometimes he came home for a quick meal before vanishing out again. I remember him coming home one evening, at about 10 o'clock, and finding me doing the ironing. He angrily told me to find enough time in the day to do such chores.

I did so, although I often had to go to coffee mornings, bridge and whist drives, not to play but to help serve teas, all in aid of the Party.

However, I did enjoy many of the luncheon clubs and helping at jumble sales which, with my eye for antiques, were like treasure hunts.

I didn't mind keeping the house clean and the garden tidy, but the hard work was the weekly washing. There were often 10 of Andrew's shirts, some of which had to be starched. Andrew actually once suggested that we have a housekeeper, but he never offered me a weekly charlady, as my mother-in-law had. I would never have known what to do with a housekeeper in the house all the time, as the place was not big enough for two women.

Sometimes an odd thought pestered me, that perhaps Andrew wanted someone strange in the house to frighten me off the idea of asking for a baby.

Each time I asked about starting a family, he would say, "Not in the winter – wait for the summer." And in the summer, he'd say, "Not in the summer – wait for the winter."

Then one afternoon, on a rainy October weekend, when I had again reminded Andrew how much I would like to have a child, and said that we should really start to try for one, he suddenly agreed, "All right – here, on the sofa."

I quickly looked at him, and burst out, "Oh darling, you would make me so happy!"

I tried to hug him but he gently pushed me away, saying, "Just leave your boots on."

"Why?" I thought, but I left on my new brown suede knee-length boots, and tried to shake off the bad thought that maybe he had been with long-booted prostitutes.

So after six months of marriage, my conjugal rights were fulfilled, somehow.

Later, Andrew thought of another way to stop me yearning for a child. One day, he came home with a baby poodle; a sweet fluff of white wool.

I called him Bonnie, because he was blond and French, like Bonnie Prince Charlie. Andrew guessed right; I loved him and forgot my problems, at least for a while.

I relied very much on Andrew's friendship, as I did not have a true and trusted girlfriend. I was no longer allowed to visit the people in Mrs Dixon's house because Andrew thought I was too familiar with them.

My sister-in-law, Carol, was not a friendly person. She lived in Cambridge with her husband Richard and baby Mark, who now took all her time, thoughts and interest.

Their house was a large Georgian one, and it was chaotic because Carol was not a home maker. She was a blue-stocking and proud of it, and without a daily help.

Richard didn't mind anything as long as he had his simple meals, and quietness for his own work. He had studied at Clare College, Cambridge, and become curator of a city museum.

They were very much wrapped up in their own work and world, disturbed only by our very occasional visits.

They had married at the age of 40, and a year later Carol had her baby boy. But she never asked me why I didn't have a baby.

Nobody ever asked or whispered or wondered. So I knew there was no help for me from Andrew's family – only silent avoidance.

Chapter 27

I loved Andrew very dearly and it took a lot to shake that feeling. But sometimes a little depression was creeping in, along with a hate for him, hate for being cheated, hate for seeing Carol so happy with her baby, hate for my failure to realise earlier what he was really like, for not understanding human nature and for having nobody who could have warned me about my love.

I sometimes pitied him for messing up his own life, and I pitied myself for being brought into this mess under false pretences.

I often wondered if his business partners in his office had any idea of the kind of life we led. They lived miles away, on the other side of town and out of touch. Stephen's wife was expecting her first child and Ted already had two boys.

However, we had one couple with whom we were on good terms. Christopher had a television shop that was very successful, now TV was becoming more popular. His wife Louise was charming, elegant, loving to her handsome husband, and a mother of three children.

They had a nice over-furnished and over-decorated house near us. They were our constant companions when we went to dine in various restaurants and pubs in Warwickshire.

How I enjoyed these jolly evenings, and Andrew was always in a wonderfully relaxed mood after a strenuous day's work.

We even went on a long holiday together, to the South of France, driving our own cars. We took the journey slowly, staying in good and bad hotels in France.

On our way to Geneva, in the Jura mountains, the windscreen wipers on our car stopped working in pouring rain. This was the one and only time Andrew needed to try to be a handyman and invent a gadget. We tied a piece of string to the wipers, and I pulled it to operate them until we arrived in Geneva. We enjoyed the day's rest there, and even the car felt better after the repairs.

We drove to Grasse via the Route Napoleon, hardly daring to glance at the beautiful mountain view because of the sheer drop at the side of the road.

I wanted to relieve Andrew from the hours of concentration by doing some of the driving myself. I felt very confident, and was happy to lead ahead of Christopher and Louise, but Christopher didn't agree. He wanted to lead. I had learned a long time before that men didn't really like women drivers. At least, I thought, Christopher would feel less nervous if I was driving behind as he couldn't see what I was doing.

Picnics on the journey, especially high up in the mountains with a fabulous view, were so enjoyable and restful that one could almost go on holiday for that reason alone.

Loaded with, and smelling of, various perfumes, we arrived in Cannes in time for dinner. It was high season, and our hotel wasn't the best in town. Those were on the long, posh promenade, where the old French dears sipped their expensive aperitifs in the shade of the palm trees. Our hotel was behind the seaside cafés and souvenir shops, with a view onto the back street.

Inside, with its bare tiled floor and polished brown furniture, any sound echoed. It looked as if it didn't matter if you came in with bare feet and sand between your toes, wearing a dripping swimming costume. The hotel seemed to be quite used to it.

We had glorious weeks in Juan-le-Pins, mostly lying on the beach on hired sun mats under large umbrellas, like thousands of other tourists.

It was different from our previous summer holiday, when we had been in St Austell, Cornwall, with only a doctor, his wife and dog sharing the beach with us.

Here in the hot sun, we had laughter all the time with Christopher and Louise. We even laughed when we started to look pink and sunburnt, when speeding along on pedalos and falling off them, and especially when Andrew was trying to teach Louise to swim. Then all the other sunbathers joined in the hilarity.

We had our aperitifs in the beach cafés, and our dinners in very French restaurants. We went to a nightclub and saw a fabulous show while sipping champagne. Later, I saw the same showgirls in their wonderful dresses, parading in town, and I heard people saying they were all men.

I wonder where I would have ended up if I had hopped into a gorgeous open-topped sports car when it stopped in front of me, as I was crossing the road in my bikini, and the driver said, "Come and join us. Just hop in now."

Instead, I managed to drag us all to Vallauris and its art gallery, where Picasso was living at that time.

I didn't pester Andrew about a baby, but I did notice one day that he wanted to make Christopher and Louise think that there was love-making in our room too.

We'd had our rest after lunch, and were about to leave our room to go and meet them at the agreed time, when Andrew suddenly said, "Stop. Let's stay here for a few minutes, quietly."

I asked him why but he didn't answer.

Our slow journey back through France was such a joy to my traveller's spirit, seeing and exploring new villages and towns.

We left Juan-le-Pins in the early morning, but as we were driving along the Cote d'Azure, near St Raphael, we suddenly saw Christopher driving back towards us. We all stopped and he explained that he'd left his false teeth under the bed!

Again, we spent several nights in France as we took a different route home. It didn't matter how poor the hotel looked – they were all equipped for modern living, with central heating and a bidet in the bathroom. Triumphantly, I pointed this out to Andrew, but he wasn't impressed. It was all too French for him.

Louise couldn't forget the hotel's facilities either. Later, when we were back home and together at a cocktail party, I heard her talking about our holiday.

She was saying, "All the hotels had such good amenities but of course we didn't need the bidet as we already had a toilet in our bathroom."

I quickly pulled her away from the group and explained what a bidet was for.

"Oh fancy! I didn't know that," she said, and rejoined the group. A couple of minutes later, I heard her talking to a different group about our holiday.

"Of course, we didn't need the bidet as we had a toilet in our bathroom," she said.

I didn't know about the strong feelings between English and French people, but I soon noticed that there was no love lost between them. It often looked as if they were still at war, but without the arms.

Christopher and Andrew had a reasonable command of French and tried to explain the subtle insults that were quietly exchanged at the hotel restaurants.

Sometime later, I had another chance to go to France, this time for a week in Paris with our Conservative women's group. Andrew's partner's wife and a couple of other young women were with us, but otherwise the coach was full of elderly ladies. We still had a hectic week, though.

We usually delivered the elderly ladies back to the hotel early, and then we younger ones were taken to late-night shows and breakfast at Les Halles. We loved it all, despite sleeping only around ten hours in the whole week.

Another politically busy winter came and went. I didn't complain any more about my childlessness. It didn't seem to be worth getting upset and weepy about it.

There was my daily life with all its work and problems, and there was Andrew's political career to worry about. We had so many ladies' nights, dinner dances, cocktail parties and political functions to attend, that evening dresses and appearances became an important and time-consuming worry.

I loved that dancing life, although I often had to go and find my own company as Andrew always disappeared to the bar, leaving me alone. Luckily, I usually found someone who wanted to tell me about their problems or happiness, children or holidays.

Perhaps if these events had continued all my life, they would have become boring, but I was happily excited to have my picture in the papers and people stopping me in the street to tell me they knew who I was. Sometimes, they wanted to know more about me and if I had any children. I managed not to look too unhappy when I told them I didn't have a family, but inside I was very jealous of all young mothers, who never seemed to stop talking about their little ones. I was often so desperately sore that I promised myself I would never baby-sit for anyone.

Another summer came and went, and we were going on holiday to Salcombe, Devon, to an exclusive little gourmet hotel where they didn't allow young children. We were having a wonderful rest, with swimming and walking to try to minimise the effects of our daily seven-course dinners.

Then one day, someone appeared in the dining room, saying, "Hello! How nice to see you here!"

It was our private doctor Henry who, with his wife, was booked into the hotel for our second week. I hadn't met Henry's wife before, although they lived in a large house near us.

211

We dined together that evening and other evenings, too. Although they were much older than us, we walked together over the hills and laughed and swam in the hotel's warm, sunny bay. It was a wonderful and interesting holiday, as we got to know and enjoy each other's company.

Late autumn brought with it the deadly Asian flu. I caught it rather badly and stayed in bed for several days. Andrew said he was too busy to catch it, but had kindly asked Henry to pop in to see me.

I was in bed when Henry rang the door bell. I went to let him in, and he ordered me back to bed, saying the house wasn't warm enough to lounge about in. He examined me and wrote out a prescription, but didn't seem to be in a hurry to go. He sat for quite a while on my bed and looked at me very seriously. Then he asked, "Kaisu, what is wrong with your marriage?"

Now it was my turn to look at him. I blushed and a couple of tears rolled down my cheek as I asked him what he meant.

"Anybody can see that there is something wrong with your life," he said. "I saw it all on holiday in Salcombe. Andrew behaves strangely. He doesn't help you, ever. He avoids you as much as he can. I don't think he even notices you."

I knew it was all true, even though I'd tried to think it was the English way of marriage and that I shouldn't make a fuss about it.

I had come to accept it. But I hadn't forgotten that Andrew would never help me – even on dark, rainy evenings, when I was trying to hold up the hem of a long dress and keep an umbrella open as well, Andrew wouldn't ever come to open the car door for me or help in any other way. I didn't mention it to Andrew but I quietly despised him for this behaviour.

"No, I'm not happy at all," I confessed to Henry. "I don't even feel married. We don't make love. It's happened only five times in all these years, and he always wears protection so we can't have children. I married him for love and to have a family."

I told Henry how, after being married for six months, we had at last made love. Afterwards, in a moment of passion, I had hugged Andrew and kissed him hard. He had gone rigid and pushed me away, saying in tones of horror, "Don't ever do that again."

My smile had vanished and I could only ask, "But why? Why can't I kiss you when I love you so much and you are my husband?"

After that, the kisses had become very small and formal, and were getting more rare until the only ones were in my memory.

Now I started to cry.

"I have never told anyone about this," I said to Henry. "Nobody has ever asked me and I don't know anyone who I could talk to anyway."

"Oh Kaisu. This is just what I feared," said Henry. "This kind of marriage is no good for anybody, either for their physical or mental state. Tell me all about it and I'll come to see Andrew tonight for a long talk."

He held my hand.

"Thank you, Henry," I wept. "Sometimes I think I'm going to have a nervous breakdown. I'm sure it'll come one day."

Poor Henry was obviously quite shocked about the state of our marriage, and he wanted to know all about our relationship and Andrew's everyday behaviour. I told him that Andrew sometimes went to Brighton – alone, he told me – for the weekend and even on a cruise in the Mediterranean. He once went to America.

I remembered Andrew's childhood friend Moira popping in one day when he was away on a cruise.

213

"Why are you here? Why aren't you with him, you fool?" she nearly shouted.

"He didn't want me there. I'm looking after Bonnie," I told her.

"Don't you dare do that next time," she told me. "You must go with him. He has no right to go without you. Remember that."

I felt wonderful after her shouting, but the next time never came. Now I felt wonderful again after talking to Henry, unburdening myself of worry and sadness. Finally, I said to him, "I'm glad you're going to talk to Andrew, but I'm sure he won't like it."

"Don't worry – it'll be for his own good," Henry responded, squeezing my hands in farewell.

All the same, I was worried about the coming explosion, but it never happened.

Andrew wasn't very late that evening, and listened quietly about Henry's intended visit. I also told him that Henry was worried about our marriage. Perhaps I sounded pleased that someone had noticed the problems. And Henry wasn't an outsider – he was our doctor and worried about his patients.

Finally, Andrew said quietly, "I won't see him," and went downstairs.

There wasn't long to wait before I heard the doorbell, then brief, unclear words and the front door closed.

Andrew didn't come upstairs to tell me what had happened, but later, when I went down to make a little supper, he curtly answered my question.

"I threw him out," he said.

We never discussed Henry again, or ever saw him. Andrew kept control of me, and I suppose that I was a bit afraid of him so I tried hard to be a good English wife to him.

Chapter 28

After Henry, we had our ordinary friendly and talkative Jewish doctor to see us if needed. However, Andrew relied mainly on his consultant friends and I was happy with that as I had a secret fear of approaching breakdown.

Luckily, it never came, although one day I found myself in the woods behind our garden, sitting on a tree trunk and crying. I was crying alone in desperation, just as I had cried after my family had been killed in the bombing.

I couldn't stop crying. I had been in the woods for hours and was getting cold. I slowly realised that Andrew would have come home for dinner. I walked through the garden and saw him standing indoors, looking out at me.

I walked in with my hot and swollen face. Still sobbing and absolutely worn out, I sat down. He was standing there, looking at me silently and without asking any questions.

"I'm so unhappy," I sobbed to him, begging for his understanding.

Suddenly, he lifted his arm, and still without saying a word, hit me hard on the side of the head. I nearly fell off the chair. Without waiting to see the result of his shock action, he marched out and left me to recover and prepare our silent supper.

After that, of course, he avoided me by staying in his study, and I cried myself to sleep in bed on my own. None of this was mentioned again, until much later in the High Court.

Shortly after this, we were visiting friends for dinner. I was in the toilet when, to my horror, I started to bleed badly. It stopped after a while, and although nobody asked why I'd spent so much time away from the table, I told Andrew about it on the way home.

The bleeding never happened again, but Andrew booked me in to see a specialist. At Andrew's request, the doctor admitted me to hospital for ten days.

Andrew kept my hospital stay a secret so that no-one came to see me, probably fearing that I'd talk too much. Andrew was the only person who came, hurriedly, a couple of times.

Once, a surgeon friend of ours, who had seen my name on the list, came to cheer me up and didn't ask any serious questions.

Luckily, I was quite well in hospital, so there was no need to have the horrible electroconvulsive therapy that was given to other patients in my ward. I had a feeling that even the nurses were baffled about the reason for my stay.

Andrew's parents were told that I'd been in hospital only after I was back home again, and the subject was never mentioned after that. Perhaps they were just as puzzled about it as I was.

I was beginning to realise, though, that I felt better when I was away from Andrew. I wasn't ill. I was only unhappy.

Life soon settled back into the old routine. In the mornings, I cooked breakfast for Andrew, and if I needed the car I drove him to the station to catch the train into town.

Andrew's parents often came for Sunday lunch. I enjoyed their visits, especially as they liked the roast lunches so much. We'd have a drink beforehand, to celebrate the weekend, if nothing else.

One lovely Sunday, Andrew's parents were again sitting at the table, waiting while Andrew and I were in the kitchen carving the beef. Andrew was sharpening the knife with a big steel. He was doing it fiercely, with a look of anger on his face.

I suddenly realised he was coming closer and closer to me.

"Andrew, you're going to hurt me soon. You're too near me," I said in alarm, stepping back and looking at his staring eyes.

He stopped and threw down the steel and knife. They landed on the roast and then all of it fell on the floor. Without a word, Andrew turned and went upstairs.

Quietly, I picked up the meat, wiped it, cleaned the floor and went into the dining room. I looked at Andrew's parents' questioning faces, and knew they must have heard what had happened.

"Andrew has gone upstairs," I told them. "I'll carve the meat and we'll have our lunch."

His mother lowered her head, as if in shock, but she recovered and we finished our lunch without talking about the incident.

When Andrew came down to join us much later, I asked him, "Why did you do that?" I didn't ask him if he was all right; I left that to his parents.

He eventually said that he was well and wanted to drive them home. I don't know what reason he gave them for his behaviour, but the subject was taboo between us.

That summer, we spent another strange holiday, this time in Spain. We didn't go to a popular resort, but to a little village hotel near Palamos. The only other guests in the hotel were a young English family with three little children, and three English men – Andrew told me they were Post Office workers.

They all shared the long empty beach with us, with the Guardia Civil coming each day on their motorbikes to check that no bikinis were being worn.

With the young family, we hired a taxi and made a hot day trip to Gerona. Andrew and I also went by taxi to Barcelona. There was so much to see – the flamenco dancers, the architecture and the shops – so we were glad to have a rest and a long lunch. Then we went to a bullfight, which was an interesting Spanish cultural event.

The evenings in our hotel were quiet. The young family went upstairs early with their children, and the three men went into the bar with Andrew.

He asked me to go to bed early each evening, to read my book, while he stayed downstairs with the three men. I never heard him coming up to our bedroom although he was always there in the morning.

It never dawned on me what was wrong with our marriage, with Andrew or perhaps with me. Not until the day I ran away to London, and to Andrew's empty flat in his Kensington house.

The flat was in a lovely four-storey property that he'd bought as an investment a couple of years earlier. Most of it was let, and the basement flat was occupied by two women, Edith and Patricia, who kept the house in order for him.

I'd never seen the house but knew where it was. So one lovely summer day, when life was quiet without any important commitments, I packed a few things and took a train to London.

I had no keys, but I introduced myself to Edith and Patricia, who showed me to Andrew's empty but furnished flat where I could stay.

While I was talking to them, I really felt that I'd at last done something very daring, that would show Andrew how little I cared for his odd attitude and how well I could manage in London.

At that moment, of course, he didn't know what I'd done – I wondered if he'd trouble to find out, or to tell the police, but if he did that everybody would know I'd run away and he couldn't possibly face that.

I found some shops nearby and bought some food, and I had supper alone in the flat. Then I went down to the basement to see Edith and Patricia. They were very friendly and helpful, and even offered me a sofa to sleep on, in case I felt lonely upstairs.

Then I saw that there was only one bed – a double bed – in their flat. Suddenly I understood everything. They were lesbians, and I even saw Patricia, the smaller one, wearing men's pyjamas.

All this was very new to me – they were the first lesbians I'd ever knowingly met and they were perfectly nice, ordinary people. They even worried about my having left Andrew without telling him where I was. They thought I should ring him and say I was safe.

I did so that same evening. It was late and he was at home.

"Hello Andrew. You've probably wondered about me," I said to him. "I'm in London in your Kensington flat and I'm all right. How are you?"

That was all I said, although I'd have liked to unburden myself of my unhappiness.

"It's good that you're safe. Now have a few days there and a good rest," he told me. "I think you've got enough money for a while. We'll see then what we'll do next. I'll ring you in a couple of days' time. All right? Goodbye then."

Andrew obviously didn't miss me at all. Perhaps he was even glad that I'd gone and he was able to have a rest from me. I thought, later, that it would be an easy solution to his problems if I stayed in London.

He didn't ring me but he did write a short letter, with a polite request that I use an advertisement that he enclosed, for a dating bureau, where I could find myself male company.

So he wanted me to find someone else, but was it for this holiday or forever? How could he do this?

I didn't want to think that he really wanted to part from me. He might, perhaps, if I was leaving him for someone else, but I couldn't do that – I loved him too much. He didn't have another woman, I was sure. So could it be a man? But who? I knew only that he'd got someone else. And that he was gay.

A friend had recently told me that, in a men-only restaurant, Andrew had put his hand on his thigh, which had horrified him. Perhaps this London trip had been

219

necessary for me to see things in a clear light, in the same way that I now knew he was gay.

I had only once, in Finland, heard about homosexuality, when an old school friend told me that she had broken her engagement with someone because he was gay. I remember being so surprised about that word that I daren't ask anything in case I revealed my ignorance.

I blamed myself for being so stupid and ignorant about sexual matters that I hadn't seen the signs with Andrew until it was too late. I just had to start to understand him and accept him as he was.

But what about me? I'd been dragged into this marriage under false pretences, promised "nine or eleven children" in Andrew's love letter to me in Finland. And now I couldn't even mention children, love or sex without him saying, "Oh hell, not that again. Wait until next winter and we'll think about it then."

I'd tried to get into his bed, whispering, "Darling, I love you so. Cuddle me."

"Oh hell, go away," he told me.

I'd crept back to my bed and cried silently while he slept. Our beds remained virgin beds all our married life.

I used my few days in London to explore Kensington, and found wonderfully sophisticated houses and calm squares. Once, I passed the open door of an empty-looking house and cheekily asked the policeman standing at the door if the house was for sale. No it wasn't, he said, but I could go in and have a look at it. To my surprise, I found two more policemen upstairs, keeping an eye on the street. They were expecting something to happen. I never found out what it was.

My return home was as outwardly dull as my life was inwardly. I had to bury my threatening depression. I pretended to everyone that everything was all right, and I lied about my happiness.

I concentrated my energies on work and politics, which meant Andrew was happy about me and didn't worry about our situation. There never seemed to be a chance to talk about ourselves – our lives revolved around formal and official comings and goings.

But my optimistic attitude had been shaken. What purpose did I have in life, I often wondered. Perhaps there were people who talked about us, or even worried about us, but I couldn't go and ask them.

So I decided to take the initiative and go and talk to Andrew's parents.

I rang the doorbell and Andrew's mother answered. She welcomed me with a smile, as she always did so sweetly.

"Come in my dear. We're going to have tea now. I hope you have time to have a cup with us," she said.

"No thank you," I replied. "This time, I just want to come and talk to you about Andrew and me."

I followed her into the living room, where Andrew's father was sitting with a book.

"Are you alright, my dear?" Andrew's mother asked.

His father put his book on the table by his side and looked at me with a worried expression on his face.

"Yes, I'm alright, thank you," I said. "I wanted to come to talk to you because I'm sure you've been thinking, or even worrying, about why we have no children after so many years.

"I can tell you that it's nothing to do with me. I would love to have children. I love Andrew and I married him to have a family – he promised me this, in writing – and I planned to live happily ever after with him. But this hasn't happened.

"At first, I couldn't understand why not, but now I can tell you that Andrew doesn't want children, nor does he want to make love or to have any kind of married life.

"I'm desperately unhappy, but I'm sure you knew all about it better than me, and you know why he behaves towards me as he does.

"I don't think there is very much hope for us. I just have to accept it, I suppose, as well as I can."

I paused as I saw Andrew's mother's face becoming red and tears starting to run down her cheeks. She didn't say a word, nor did Andrew's father. She rose from her chair, and covering her face, she left the room. I heard her going up the stairs.

I looked at Andrew's father's unhappy face, whispered "Goodbye" and walked out of the house.

Chapter 29

I wandered the streets for a long time, near the church where I had been married so many years before, and when I had been full of hope and happiness and so proud of Andrew.

I was still in love with him. I respected him above all, and I still had a little flicker of hope that all would be better one day, especially now that I'd told his parents about our situation. Surely they'd tell Andrew about my visit?

The only problem was that Andrew was their god and they wouldn't dare to criticise him. And would anything really change him?

Later that evening, after our meal and our chat about the day's work, I told Andrew I'd seen his parents and told them about our life. He didn't ask any questions or make any comments. He didn't cry like his parents. He just stiffened and looked at me as though he'd seen a ghost – just as he'd done after our wedding, when he'd realised his mistake.

He looked as though he wanted to say, "How dare you?" but he stayed silent. He just got up, quietly, and went to the study. He never said anything about it and I never knew what, if anything, his parents had said to him.

Later, I realised that, from that time on, he started to think that I was a danger to him, even though I hadn't mentioned the word "homosexual" to his parents.

But would I tell someone else that he was gay? And would the papers find out about his habits, which were illegal at that time? If so, what would happen to his political life and his future?

It all spelled disaster for him, personally and for his career, and the outcome would be prison.

I didn't want to hurt him. I only wanted him to know that I now knew. Knowledge was like an ace in my hand. He knew it, too, and he was afraid of it.

All the same, I wasn't interested to find out where he'd been or what he'd done, because even in a politically quiet time he would always have come out with the same answer – work.

All his time outside home was work. I wasn't allowed to check this as he'd told me never to phone him in his office, so I never did – never in all those years or even during a crisis when I might have needed help.

I also had my own life and future to consider. Andrew's parents' attitude to me didn't change, nor mine to them, but I felt that there was now a little underlying sadness at our meetings. Perhaps our joy and enthusiasm for life had vanished and harsh reality had stepped in.

Was this how the future would be for all of us, or were we waiting and hoping that Andrew would change? None of us knew, and we all kept our guesses to ourselves.

There was another disappointment when Andrew lost in the Parliamentary elections. It was a Labour seat and we'd not expected much. However, he did very well because he got the Labour vote down much lower than the national average. It was his first attempt – a learning experience – and he was ready to try again, with better luck in a better constituency.

Following the busy weeks of electioneering, the counting of votes in the town hall made for an exciting evening and night, especially at the end when the winners were announced by the Lord Mayor of the city.

The hall was filled with long tables and there were dozens of people sorting the voting slips into small piles, which were then examined and counted by the people sitting round the tables. A lot of us were walking around and keeping an eye on the counters.

It reminded me of a previous election count, when I'd happened to stop behind one man who was flicking the slips. Suddenly, he'd paused. There on the voting slip, in bold writing, was "f*** off".

"What does that mean," I'd asked the man.

He had turned slowly towards me, looked at me for a long time, then turned back and started counting.

I had asked Andrew about the words on the voting slip. He was standing with Birmingham's Lord Mayor and the Deputy Mayor, both beautifully dressed with their chains of office. Poor Andrew got such a shock from my question that he blushed and angrily told me never to use that word again. The mayors had a hearty laugh.

When the elections were over, we went for a relaxing evening with Christopher and Louise to a new restaurant in Warwickshire. Louise and I were in the ladies room when she mentioned babies.

Casually she asked me, "Any sign of yours?"

"No, of course not," I answered.

"Oh. Why, what's the matter?" Louise asked.

"Andrew doesn't want any children. Louise, I can't tell you any more. You have to guess. Please let's go."

I was nearly crying.

Louise put her arm round my shoulders and hugged me all the way back the table.

"I'd guessed," she said, softly, but she never again referred to it.

Years later, just after Christopher had died, Andrew had said to her, "You'll get over it soon."

Louise had started shouting at him.

"How can you say that?" she had asked him, furiously. "You don't know what love or loving is. You've never loved anybody but yourself."

She told me about this conversation with Andrew years afterwards, when we were talking on the phone.

We also made new young friends – Stuart and Angela – who lived near us in a big house with four adopted children and three dogs.

As usual, they were planning a skiing holiday with their friends in Switzerland, and they asked me to join them. Of course, I was very keen to go. I had skied all my life – probably before I could walk – and I was going to enjoy this holiday.

We stayed at the Grand Hotel, in Leysin, which had its own station at the highest point at the end of a little electric railway line. We spent the days on the slopes, and on the way back to the hotel we'd stop in the village for cocoa and enormous cream cakes.

In the evenings, after dinner – for which we dressed up – we left the old duchesses playing cards in the grand lounge with its beautiful chandeliers, oriental carpets and shining parquet floors.

We spent the late evenings in the downstairs piano bar, where the pianist played as long as there was at least one couple on the dance floor.

Sometimes, we swapped dinner for a fondue party in a room next to the piano bar, and ate and danced all night. We laughed about our skiing, and in the ladies room compared the blue bruises on our bottoms, which looked just like colourful maps of the world.

I reminded Angela, when she had again fallen down on the slopes, that in desperation she'd shouted to her husband, "I can't play all night with you and then ski all day. You must choose now which you want me to do."

What a happy couple they were.

I got Andrew interested in this lovely relaxing winter holiday pastime, and at last he promised to come skiing with me, this time to Seefeld, Austria.

It was a big village with a skating rink, large swimming pool with saunas, and tea dances in some of the hotels. We tried all of these, because I noticed that Andrew was getting bored and bad-tempered with me as usual, even though he'd wanted to come and join me for only my second week there.

The snow was too deep for him. He kept falling into it and struggled to get up. Even the nursery slopes were too steep for him, and every time he fell over he swore instead of laughing.

It was too painful to watch him, and he never came on a skiing holiday again. It made me wonder what had happened to his sense of humour.

Another winter, I was with more friends, some of them joining us at the Grand Hotel, and we were having an hilarious time. On the last day of skiing, we returned to the hotel where I had a surprise – there was a letter for me from Andrew.

I was going to read it in my room, when I heard someone walking behind me. It was Duncan, one of our friends, whose Italian wife had just gone back to Milan.

I just had time to ask him what the matter was, when he interrupted me and said, "I came to make love to you."

"Oh no you're not," I said. "I don't like it. I don't do it, so you can go away. I've just got a letter from my husband and I want to go to my room and read it now."

He went away nicely and I hurried in to see what had happened to make Andrew write to me. The letter wasn't long, and at the end was the surprise. He'd sold our home and bought a flat in London, just as I'd always wanted, he said. He would meet me at the airport and we'd go straight to our new home, he wrote.

I was speechless with shock. I couldn't even cry. My home, that I'd had built, had gone. Another of my homes was gone. I could only repeat, "Why?"

I'd lost two homes in Finland in the bombings, then left my lodgings and my flat to come to England, so full of hope for a home of my own.

I'd never said to Andrew that I wanted to live in London. He'd lied in his letter, perhaps not only to me but also to others. How could he do it?

227

Slowly I started to understand. He couldn't afford to have me in Birmingham in case I found out more about him and started to talk. He must have planned all this for a long time, because in only two weeks you can't find a buyer for a house, choose a flat, purchase it and move there, not even if you're a lawyer.

So that was the end of our loveless marriage. The end of family meetings with Andrew's mother and father, and goodbye to all the friends we'd made.

Would they ever ask what had happened to me? Was he going to say it was all my fault? Perhaps he told them that I was one of those foreigners you can't trust – probably that I'd gone back to Finland as I was homesick.

But now I was in London, alone, knowing no-one except, vaguely, a few MPs and the Prime Minister and his wife. What a joke.

We arrived at the flat in an atmosphere of great sadness and in silence. There were so many questions I wanted to ask in the car on the way there, but I could hardly say a word.

The flat was in Highgate, in a new block with a large garden and a lovely view over Highgate Wood. It had two bedrooms, a spacious L-shaped hall, a kitchen and a living room overlooking the drive. The front garden and the street were full of very tall trees.

"I shall be here, of course, with you as much as I can once the sale of the house has gone through," said Andrew.

"Our home, my home, sold. Why? I want to know why," I interrupted, nearly crying.

Andrew continued without looking at me.

"I'm with mother and father until I get a little flat. For political reasons that's the best solution."

"And what do they say about this, about me?" I asked him.

"Nothing," said Andrew. "They understand."

Then he added, "It will be better that you never see them again. It will only upset them."

"How?" I asked, but Andrew didn't answer.

"What have you told them? I want to know," I shouted.

But he didn't answer that, either. Being a lawyer, he knew it was better to keep quiet.

"I brought nearly everything here, and was surprised at how well it all fitted," he said, after a while.

He was right about that. The whole flat seemed well furnished. Thick white carpet covered nearly all the parquet floor of the living room, and the bedrooms had fitted carpets. The curtains were perfect. The beds were just as they'd been in our old home – separated by a bedside table. All my personal things were just as I'd left them. I discovered that only my national dress was missing, never to be found.

After a cold supper, I fell asleep with shock and exhaustion. Andrew didn't sound happy either, but was clearly relieved he'd found a way to keep me quiet. Never mind how it affected me.

I was quite used to shocks in my life, but this one left me with a deep sorrow for a long time. I was in a state of limbo, not able to do much to help get myself out of it. How was I going to start living again? I don't remember much about those months.

Andrew came to the flat for the weekends, but it didn't make our life together any happier. On the contrary, he was nearly always in a filthy mood, angry and dissatisfied with everything.

He was also becoming a nervous wreck. The pressure was on in his political career, because he had been shortlisted for the Solihull constituency, which the Conservatives held with a wonderfully large majority.

But he had been thrown out by the selection committee because of a rumour that there was a problem with his marriage. Andrew's future hopes were looking shaky. But how did they know? Andrew must have told them that I wasn't available for an interview, as I should have been.

At least I tried to make our weekend dinners something special, but he hardly noticed them. His mind was always somewhere else.

One hot weekend, we discovered that there was an outdoor public swimming pool quite near us, and Andrew was very keen to try it. We were lying in the hot sun after being in the pool, when Andrew suddenly jumped up and shouted, "Hell, I can't stand this. We have to go."

He changed his clothes in a furious mood and left for Birmingham without even saying goodbye to me.

Chapter 30

However, something nice and exciting often happens, even in dark times.

In the early 1960s, I received a letter from Buckingham Palace, inviting us to a garden party. There was plenty of time to prepare for it and I decided to make the most of it.

At Harrods, I found a lovely Dior dress and coat, but they were far too big for me. At Fortnum & Mason, I found a lovely outfit, but it was in dark brown. Liberty didn't have anything suitable either, but they did have pink Thai silk – I bought a length and copied the Dior dress and coat. With pink shoes, long white gloves, and a white hat with a veil and large pink rose, I was ready to curtsy to the Queen.

It happened to be a special garden party, as it coincided with a conference of Commonwealth prime ministers in London – they were all at the party, along with only half as many other guests compared with the numbers invited nowadays. Even the weather was perfect.

We parked the car on The Mall and excitedly walked to the gates, where a small crowd of people was standing watching the arrivals. There was only one other couple going in at the same time as us – Douglas Fairbanks Jnr and his wife – and people were kindly applauding.

Tea was served, the band played, and the Queen and her family walked along slowly, greeting, smiling and talking to her guests. I had an even better view of her later, in the tent with her dignitaries. What better place to do some people-watching than a Royal garden party?

As we left, on our way through the big hall, I asked a footman where the ladies' toilets were. I was shown a door, and beyond was a long corridor with lots of doors to various rooms full of furniture, but I never found the ladies' toilets.

The day had brought me other joy as well. In the morning, as we were leaving our flat, we stood outside the front door taking photos. Suddenly, a man walked out of the door, greeted Andrew and asked what he was doing there.

"Hello Rowland," said Andrew. "I live here and this is my wife, Kaisu."

Don explained that he and his wife Margaret were staying with his aunt, in the same block of flats as ours, while their house was being decorated.

Andrew later told me that he and Rowland had been at the same Cambridge College.

Soon afterwards, Rowland and Margaret came to visit us, along with Rowland's Aunt Iris. I liked them very much; Rowland became my doctor and Iris a very special friend. She was about my mother's age, and the widow of an RAF pilot who, when he was younger, had tried to fly around the world but had crashed and wrecked his plane. Both Iris's boys joined the RAF, but the younger one died at the age of 51, when he was an air vice-marshal.

Iris became like a mother to me, until her death 16 years later. I felt that I was like a missing daughter to her, as she cared and worried about me.

There were other people in the block of flats with whom I became great friends. I was particularly fond of the children who lived next door. They were the little sons of an Iraqi doctor – descendants of the original Iraqi Christian families – and they had red hair and very white skin.

I loved these boys and often felt they were half mine as I continued to long for my own child. These boys are now both surgeons with families of their own.

Gradually, I became more familiar with my friends who lived in our block, and they started to insist that I divorce Andrew. They even found me a lawyer.

By that time, Andrew and I had become strangers. Weekends were formal drinks and dinner occasions, with Andrew busily talking about work and politics but never asking me about my life or friends.

Soon after coming to London, I received an invitation to a wedding in Birmingham. Andrew forbade me ever to go to that city again, but I went anyway and enjoyed the weekend very much.

Apparently, Andrew had been so frightened by this that he'd had to leave the city altogether. After that, I never went to Birmingham again, and never saw my friends or Andrew's family.

Andrew bought me a car – one of the first Minis – that I kept for 16 years, and it became my best friend. Now I was mobile, I decided to go to Cambridge to tell Carol all about our marriage.

It was a beautiful spring morning as I drove through the lovely quiet countryside, thinking about how much I would shock Carol and Richard with my story. I was sure that, if they knew only a fraction of the truth, they would probably blame me for the break.

Luckily, Carol was alone when I got to the house. We sat together on a sofa, and in just a few sentences I told her what had happened. She didn't seem surprised, and I still don't know if she accepted, or even realised, that Andrew was gay. She was more concerned to tell me at length about her own unhappiness, which came as a surprise to me.

She blamed her parents even more than she blamed Andrew for ignoring her, sometimes even hating her and leaving her to battle with her studies without any help. She was obviously still very jealous of Andrew, whom her parents had always adored and helped. She couldn't stop crying. I held her in my arms, trying to comfort her and dry her tears.

After two hours and a quick lunch, I drove back to London. Though she was a keen letter-writer, I never received any letters from her or any of the family, and I never wrote to them either.

Now I was again without a family, I was very glad to get a call from Hilary, in Paris, inviting me to spend 10 days with her, while her husband, Edward, was in Africa.

Edward was Andrew's old Cambridge friend, and the boss of a big oil company in the French-speaking part of the world. Andrew wasn't keen for me to go, but I accepted the invitation anyway.

Hilary's home was in the best part of Paris – a most gorgeous flat, reminding me of Versailles with its mirrored doors. A lovely Spanish couple took care of us. How I enjoyed being pampered and chauffeured about town.

We went to a big party given by a British Embassy couple, Timothy and Stephanie, who later became great friends of mine when they came to live in Highgate.

The party started with a dinner, after which we all went to the Lido show and then back to the house for a late supper. After the party was over, in the small hours, we started to walk down the grand white marble staircase. I slipped, but as I was still holding the handrail, I started to slide down the stairs still standing up.

When I reached the bottom, I realised both my high heels had been left behind on the top step. What a fitting end to an hilarious party! Someone took me in his arms and carried me to the car, to the sound of laughter and clapping. And after a half-crown heel mend, my shoes were still lovely.

We had another unforgettable party at the home of the British Ambassador, Sir Pierson Dixon. I heard about it when Stephanie was with us at Pierre Balmain's fashion show. I overheard Hilary whispering to Stephanie, "Do you think I could take Kaisu to the Sewells', as Edward is away?"

"Of course," replied Stephanie.

But at her home, Hilary panicked. "You don't have a cocktail hat," she said to me.

"But you have some lovely veils," I replied, "and if Clements can drive me to the Gallerie Lafayette, I will get some roses. You see – it'll be all right."

I found some gorgeous red silk roses, which I sewed onto Hilary's beautiful black net veil. It came half-way down my face. With my hair up and in my little black dress, I felt good. At the door, Lady Sewell greeting me with, "My dear! Where did you get such a wonderful hat?"

On the way home afterwards, in the back seat of her limousine, Hilary kept repeating one of the nicest compliments; "I just can't understand Andrew – how can he leave you?"

I now had lots of time on my hands, and asked Andrew if I could go on a cruise. Why shouldn't I have pleasure trips, I thought, just as he'd had without me? Andrew was very willing to agree, so I joined the Andes on her cruise in the Mediterranean. She was an old ship, and had even been in the war, and this was one of her last voyages before being scrapped. There were more crew than passengers, and we were all one class, so were very well cared for.

On the first evening, at the captain's cocktail party, someone gathered the younger passengers together, so we started the holiday with some memorably lively parties, and forged friendships that still endure.

We stopped in Lisbon, Palma, Rhodes, Alexandria and Israel, and had time to explore most of them. I still remember the awful headache I had while driving down to the Sea of Galillee, which is 200 metres below sea level.

In Cairo, a friend wanted to pay a return visit to the best dentist in the country. We searched for this dentist all over Cairo. He turned out to be a large and prosperous-looking man, and we found him in his surgery with his apprentice – a 10-year-old boy who was cleaning the instruments.

Another friend took me to a belly-dancing hall. There was a band and a lot of men standing around watching the colourful dancers, who performed to the loud, hectic music. We were the only tourists there.

Soon, a young girl came to our table.

"What's your name?" asked my friend.

"Whisky please," was the answer.

She didn't know any more words, except "Greek".

In Alexandria, we visited King Farouk's palace, which had been left untouched since his death.

It was my first trip outside Europe, and I had been bitten by the travel bug.

The following year, Andrew sent me on two more cruises. Aboard the Agamemnon, I sailed around Greece. As we left the Corinth Canal, we happened to sail alongside Aristotle Onassis's floating palace, the Christina. It was huge.

I was thrilled by the Acropolis, which seemed to be far beyond comparison with other temples.

My table companions were Viscount David Greenwood and his carer – a male teacher. As a child, poor David had been dropped by his nanny and was still mentally young. He had an all-in-one stripy swimming costume, which amused everybody.

My other cruise was in a banana boat, the Camito, to the West Indies. Her captain was Lucky Lundi – a very strict war-time hero, who kept his ship in perfect order. He kept me under his protection, and I became his dinner companion.

I was lucky to have the use of Princess Alice's cabin. For part of the cruise, we had important visitors: Lord Patrick Buchan-Hepburn, 1st Baron Hailes, who was Governor General of the West Indies Federation, plus his family and staff. They were on an official visit from

Trinidad to Kingston. I moved from the captain's table to make way for them, but was pleased to be invited to their parties.

Although it was autumn, Kingston was still very humid, which added to the discomfort of the official greetings and presentations.

I was watching the band playing at the harbour, and saw how wonderfully graceful and cool Lady Hailes looked in her elegant dress, hat and long gloves, and her husband in uniform and with feathers in his hat.

Like so many English people, they had been well trained to carry out their duties graciously. Lady Hailes's tip to me for keeping cool was to drop all thoughts, except the most important one for that moment.

After this, the ship went round the islands collecting unripe bananas. They were carried on the backs of women – all wearing colourful dresses – and along a plank to the cold hold of the ship.

In Jamaica, I was invited to visit a prosperous banana planter's house. It was a lovely white colonial building, its elegance matching that of the host and hostess, with their small children who were cared for by a Jamaican mammy.

We went to the Blue Mountain Inn for a dinner dance, all in evening dresses. Princess Margaret had recently been dancing there too. The night was black, and when the band stopped playing, we could hear the frogs croaking on the muddy road up to the inn.

By contrast, we also enjoyed the local barbecue, with planters' punches, limbo dancers and ecstatic singing and drumming, lasting all night.

Chapter 31

Back home to reality, the divorce came to me like a death –
or even worse than a death. I still loved Andrew, and kept
his picture on my bedside table, long after we separated.

The case was in the High Court, and was done quietly
so the newspapers wouldn't notice. My counsel said he'd
never heard of such a case.

Of course, I was nervous standing in the witness box
and giving the details of our marriage. Andrew wasn't in
court, so there was no case for the defence.

After the verdict, I took Iris – who had been in court
with me – for lunch at the Savoy. Though it was winter, the
weather outside the big windows looked sunny and hopeful,
with spring rushing in. Inside, we enjoyed a delicious lunch
and I felt cautiously optimistic about the future.

However, on the night before the divorce became
absolute, Andrew had phoned me and repeatedly begged
me to cancel the action. There were still two more hours for
me to do it, but we used up all the time, talking to midnight,
and wasted the chance to halt proceedings.

I had tried for so many years to understand him, and
now I pitied him. He hadn't changed but I had grown up.

In spite of my freedom, this was one of the worst times
of my life. I had always tried not to burden my friends or
pester them, so now I spent long days alone in my quiet
flat, devoid of life, company and sympathy, divorced and
terribly lonely.

Some days, I sat for hours on the kitchen chair, looking
at the gas cooker and wondering if I should put my head in
it. I cried and cried, each time telling myself that I wouldn't
ever get as low again.

I knew I had to stop feeling sorry for myself, and
slowly I came to my senses. But the feeling of shame didn't
leave me for years.

I never volunteered the information that I was divorced. If pushed, I said that I used to be married to Andrew, who was now an MP. I never revealed the reason for the divorce, though, as I didn't want to cause problems in his new life as a junior Government minister.

What I didn't know then, though, was that Andrew had kept our marriage a great secret. Many years later, I met my own MP who had shared an office with Andrew and had had no idea he was married. He said Andrew had always let people believe he was a bachelor; and he never put my name in Who's Who? Perhaps he was afraid someone would find me and ask questions.

Now I told myself that I had to start to do something to make me "me" again. Everybody in our block of flats was working, including Iris, and so must I. But at the age of 40, and without a particular skill, what could I do?

I got in touch with the BBC World Service's Finnish section, at Bush House, and they gave me a year's contract. The Cold War was at its height and the twice-daily Finnish broadcasts were very important, as Russia jammed their own BBC output.

I had a very interesting time there, until the end of my contract. I helped to write reports about current events in England, for broadcast to Finland and Finnish-speaking Russians. A couple of times I also read out the news.

Then I went to the nearby Hornsey College of Art, to learn painting, which I had always loved. Soon, the college principal heard that I was Finnish – as he was about to go to Finland, he wanted to know about the country's artists.

Then he asked if I could help in the college library, as the librarian was ill. I loved books, so quickly agreed.

But a letter arrived from the BBC, asking me back and urging me to sign another contract. I now had a difficult decision to make.

Eventually, I chose the college, which was near my flat and where I could work only during term times. How wonderfully fate had organised my life. Hornsey College of Art was an important institution, often winning more praise and prizes than the Royal College of Art.

One rainy autumn evening in the 1960s, my doorbell rang. Waiting outside were three men. One introduced himself and a colleague as representatives of a paint company. They were looking for a flat to decorate, for free, for advertising purposes, they said, and had seen from the street that my flat was the only one in the block with the lights on.

They introduced their companion as David Hicks, son-in-law of the late Lord Mountbatten and a noted interior designer. It was pure coincidence that, when I'd first been looking for a job, I'd rung David's company with the thought that I'd like to do interior design. I'd been surprised when David answered the phone himself. Although he didn't have any vacancies, he'd asked me a little about myself, presumably because of my accent.

Now he looked round my flat and said, "We'll have an emerald green hall, pink bedroom, a pink toilet, turquoise bathroom and tomato-coloured kitchen. And you'll have new curtains and bed linen too, of course."

"No!" I said.

David had a quick think, and said: "No, a grey kitchen with a tomato-coloured back wall."

For two weeks, the Mayfair Decorating Company was hard at work, while I stayed with Iris. David came back a few times, giving me a chance to remind him about my earlier telephone call to him, while job-hunting. He kindly said that he remembered me – most likely he remembered my accent.

Photographs were taken of the flat, before and after the work was completed. The final photographs were taken on a Sunday morning. Immediately beforehand, the company "planted" hundreds of plastic daffodils in the front garden, so they gave a wonderful view from the bedroom. I had to go out and chase away the people who stopped to marvel at the out-of-season flowers.

I had made a new life for myself, and decided to make the very most of living in London. I went to exhibitions, museums, art galleries, theatres and the opera.

One year, I went to see 11 operas – not just at Covent Garden but also at Glyndebourne, where I often went with friends. Another year, three operas came to London from Finland.

I was also lucky to be able to use my Mini to visit friends in the country for long weekends. I skied in the winter, and travelled the world on long holidays. I loved it all.

I was on a skiing holiday with my neighbour, Jennifer, when I was recognised by a Birmingham councillor. She asked Jennifer about me. Afterwards, in the bar, the councillor came up to me and said they'd all been wondering what had happened to "that nice girl, Andrew's wife".

"So what did they think had happened to her?" I asked.

"They said that perhaps she went back to Finland and remarried," said the councillor.

"No, nothing like that," I said to her.

I didn't tell her the real reason for our divorce, as I didn't want to hurt Andrew's political reputation in Birmingham or the House of Commons.

My new friendship with Andrew started in Highgate, when he came to see my newly-redecorated flat. He was very formal, and he couldn't stop talking in great detail about his life in the House of Commons. I could see that he was very tense and didn't really want to meet me, but had to for his own security: he had to see what state of mind I was in because he knew I held the ace. It was a friendship that lasted until I went to live in Spain.

He didn't once ask whether I was working, or about my friends and holidays, and I didn't volunteer any information. I suggested that we should go out to dinner together, somewhere nice, like the Savoy. It was the start of our posh dinner dates that continued more or less monthly, when Parliament was sitting, until I moved to Spain.

The table booking was always left to me, and I quite often drove him back to the House for the late vote. I felt more at ease with him now than when I was married to him, and was quite often cheeky and even critical of his work in the House. He took it very well.

The House had changed him, too. He was no longer a god in the office, god at home and god in his constituency. He said the House was more like a club, and you had to learn to bear insults, too.

He was now going through the humbling stage – a stage I'd passed long before – and I had now become more confident and sure of myself.

I'd heard that Andrew was a better lawyer than he was a politician, but he did very well and had an official title for most of his time in the House. Long before his retirement, he became a Knight Bachelor.

He also remarried. One evening, just as I was about to leave my flat to go to an Anglo-Finnish Society lecture, the phone rang. A voice at the other end introduced herself as Isabel and asked to see me that evening. I recognised her name and told her I couldn't see her as I was about to go out.

"Please tell me where you're going and I'll be there," she said. "It's very important that I talk to you tonight. Just for a few minutes. Please?"

I'd heard about Isabel from my friends Edward and Hilary, who were now back from Paris. I'd spent a weekend in their gorgeous home in the country, and they told me they'd arranged to have lunch in the House with Andrew and another MP couple.

They had all met in the Central Hall, and Edward had suggested going in to eat.

"Not yet," Andrew had answered, as a lady appeared in a figure-hugging black velvet coat, with a large, shocking-pink bow at the front and wearing a large picture hat. Everyone in the hall watched in silence as she walked up to their group, and greeted Andrew, saying "Hello darling". He introduced her and they all walked in for lunch together.

It was this elegant Isabel who now awaited me that evening, when I arrived for the lecture. I couldn't see anyone else, so the young lady in a very low-cut lace dress must be her.

"Hello," she said. "I recognise you from the photographs. I'm very grateful to you for meeting me."

Then she asked if I read the Daily Mail. I told her I didn't.

"That's good because I wanted to tell you myself before you read it," she said.

She showed me her copy of the newspaper, opened it to Nigel Dempster's gossip column, and handed it to me. There was a picture of Andrew, and a separate one of Isabel, with a story about their love, hate, and engagement, which Andrew denied. Isabel said she knew who had tipped off the Daily Mail, and added that Andrew wasn't very pleased to say the least.

I was astounded. I wasn't angry – more amused about the gossip, although it wouldn't do Andrew any good.

I bought the paper the next day, and for some days to come, as the love story developed and then nearly ground to a halt when Andrew again denied that he had any intention of re-marrying. I was mentioned in the paper, too.

There was also a picture of Alice, the woman who'd tipped off the paper, and who had been waiting in vain for more than 15 years to marry Andrew.

Under pressure from the paper, Andrew eventually married Isabel and saved his reputation in the House of Commons. Alice lost everything, including an important job as matron of several large hospitals. She also lost Andrew's friendship.

She and her husband, who worked with Andrew in his legal business, had been my first friends in England. They divorced at the same time I did, and Andrew relied on Alice to "see that my mother is all right" as he told me. I never knew that she wanted to marry Andrew.

Andrew later told me that Alice had wanted to join him on a Parliamentary mission to China. Somehow, they arranged for her to travel with the mission as a representative of her own country. All was well until she heard Andrew phoning Isabel. She was so suspicious that she sent Andrew a postcard to his home in Dolphin Square – Isabel saw it and was furious that Andrew hadn't been honest with her.

This was the start of the two women's competition for Andrew's affections. Nigel Dempster's column pushed it to a happy ending for Isabel. But for Alice, it was a total emotional and financial disaster. She ended up working abroad as a children's nanny.

Like me, earlier, she blamed Andrew for destroying her life and she wrote a long article about it, with pictures taken during happier times, for a national magazine.

Chapter 32

After our first meeting, Isabel phoned me again. She wanted more information about Andrew.

She was a clever and sophisticated girl, much older than her years, and she was very keen to marry Andrew. She was an actress, and had already been in the famous comedy No Sex Please, We're British. How ironic!

The last time I saw her, she came to my home. I'd resisted a visit from her, but she insisted, promising to stay only a few minutes. She was with me for hours, talking about Andrew.

As I walked her to catch the last Tube train home, she asked the question that had been the sole reason for her visit, "Is Andrew gay?"

"Why are you asking me now," I said.

"Because he wanted to make love in the homosexual way," she replied.

I'd had that experience with Andrew, too, although I'd not realised at the time that it was a gay practice.

"Even if he is, I'm going to marry him anyway," Isabel said. "I love him and I want to have a baby with him."

"But he doesn't want to have children," I told her.

"Don't worry. I have my tricks," she assured me.

Isabel went on to marry Andrew, who was 27 years older than her. A couple of years later, they had a daughter who was pictured on Nigel Dempster's page.

Why wasn't I as clever as Isabel? The problem was that I was a foreigner without any sophistication. I hope Isabel is very happy but I also know that men don't really change.

I was still dining with Andrew after his marriage to Isabel, and he said that Isabel didn't know about our dates. I hope it was that that made him look more bewildered than happy. Silly boy.

My experience with him made me very nervous about marrying again. Not even proposals from my dear friend John Biffen – another MP and a former Conservative Cabinet Minister – could change that.

Soon after that, I went to live in Spain, which is where another chapter began in my life.

Lightning Source UK Ltd.
Milton Keynes UK
UKOW03f1045060614

232989UK00001B/2/P